Dear Ileana,

May your life be filled with God!

much gratitude,

Miriam

Praise for Miriam Grunhaus and
Heal with Gold

Inspired by the Japanese art of Kintsugi, Miriam embarked on a journey to find her own healing and ultimately joy. She has culled the wisdom of women who have thrived after tragedy and shares these lessons to heal others and guide them to a joy filled life. This book is a gem! - *Tal Ben Shahar, Founder Happiness Studies Academy, New York Times Best Selling Author of Happier*

Heal with Gold is a book about resilience written by someone who would not give in on achieving joy after hardship. Miriam uncovers the commonalities between those who succeeded in overcoming adversity and creates a visual and straightforward "How-to" Handbook for surviving adversity and thriving in joy. Read Heal with Gold and start your transformation. - *Jesse Itzler, Author "Living With A SEAL" | Co-Founder Marquis Jet | An Owner of the Atlanta Hawks | Keynote Speaker*

Everyone who succeeds does so by overcoming obstacles. It's not a matter of if we will face adversity, but it is a matter of when we will face adversity. Within these pages, Miriam takes us all on a journey from defeat to victory and shows us how we can emerge better, stronger and "victorious." - *Jim Stovall, Bestselling author, The Ultimate Gift*

Heal with Gold is full of actionable golden nuggets that will transform your life. Personally, knowing the author, I can attest to Miriam's authenticity and passion for helping women achieve joy and live a life where they not only embrace their scars, but wear them with pride, as they come to recognize that exactly what broke them is what makes them special. As a fashion designer, Miriam encapsulates this message in her collection, and this book is an extension of her work as a strong female entrepreneur who aims to uplift all in her path. – *Simonetta Lein, Top 100 fashion influencer, Activist & Founder of The Wishwall Foundation*

From victim to survivor and thriver, this beautiful uplifting book eases and supports the healing process of profound inner pain. It gives readers the courage to face adversity to mend deep-seated wounds. Like the Japanese art of Kintsugi repairs breakages with gold seams, the author reveals how to liberate yourself from adversity to reclaim your power and dignity. A "must-read" book for anyone who wants to rebuild their courage, confidence, and inner strength. – *Susan Friedmann, CSP, International Bestselling Author of Riches in Niches: How to Make it BIG in a Small Market*

Heal with Gold leads you into a personal story of you being a vase in free fall, shattering into pieces, and laying in a pain-filled mess wondering, "can I ever be whole again?" In your dust and pieces, you are desperate to be made whole again. This is Miriam's work to help you take your pieces no matter the trauma, accident, abuse, or event that caused it, and heal with gold. Why? Because you are worth it! — *April Tribe Giauque, Author of Pinpoints of Light Escaping the Abyss of Abuse, and Out of Darkness: Find, Fuel, and Live in Your Light*

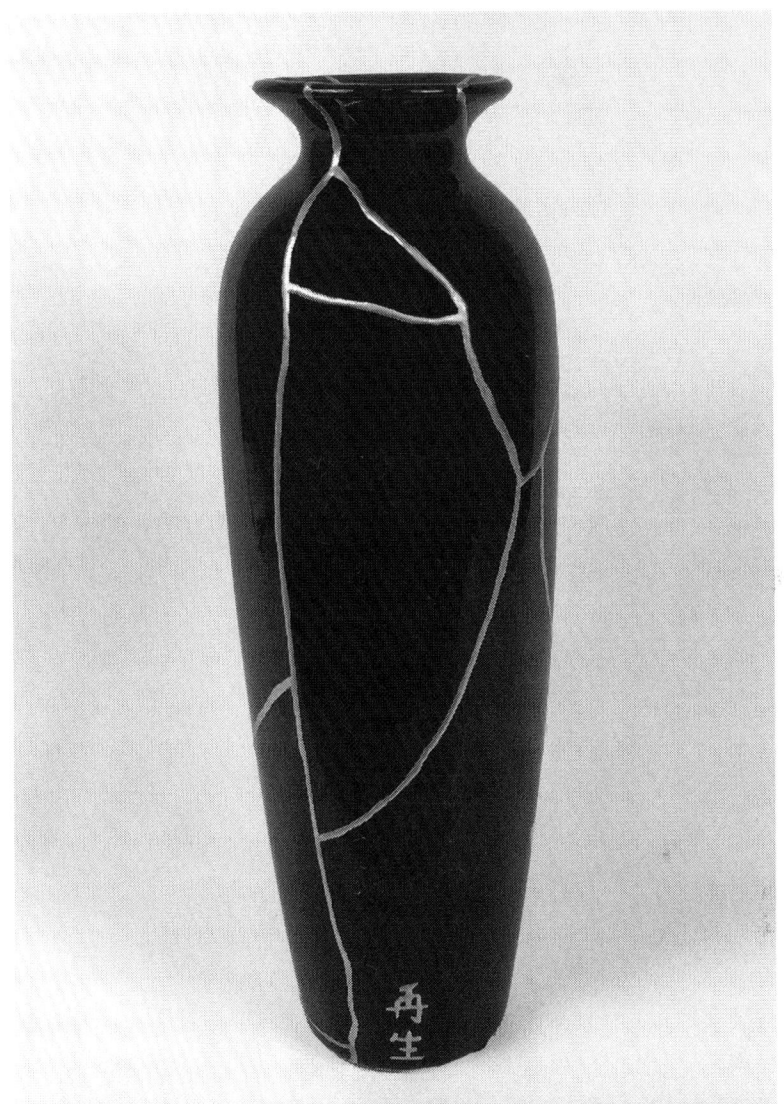

Kintsugi in Japanese means golden Joinery. This is the Japanese art of repairing broken pottery by mending the areas of breakage with lacquer and powdered gold, silver or platinum. As a philosophy, it treats breakage and repair as part of the history of an object, rather than something to disguise.

Artist: Morty Bachar, Lakeside Pottery Studio www.lakesidepottery.com

Heal with Gold © 2020 Miriam Grunhaus

For speaking inquiries, and bulk order purchase options, sales promotions, fund-raising and educational needs contact: info@healwithgold.com

All rights reserved, including the rights to reproduce this book or any portion thereof, in any form whatsoever. For information, address: info@healwithgold.com

This work is nonfiction. The author of this book does not dispense medical advice or prescribe the use of any technique, either directly or indirectly, as a form of treatment for physical, emotional or medical problems.

Name: Miriam Grunhaus, Author
Title: Heal with Gold, 10 Golden Nuggets To Heal Your Mind and Soul

Visit the author's website at www.healwithgold.com
Cover and Interior Design: Miriam Grunhaus
Author's Photo Credit: Lesley Pedraza @lesleypedraza

Library of Congress Control Number: 2020916622

Trade paperback ISBN 978-1-63618-003-8
E-Book ISBN 978-1-63618-006-9
Hardcover ISBN 978-1-63618-008-3
ePub ISBN 978-1-63618-009-0
Audiobook 978-1-63618-010-6

Aviva Publishing
Lake Placid, NY
518-523-1320
www.avivapubs.com

# Heal with Gold

10 Golden Nuggets to
Heal Your Mind and Soul

# Heal with Gold

## 10 Golden Nuggets to Heal Your Mind and Soul

### Miriam Grunhaus

AVIVA
PUBLISHING
New York

# DEDICATION

*I dedicate this book to all who have experienced loss of the living.
I hear you. I see you. I feel you.
You are not alone.*

---

*I was raised in a home where there were no walls without bookshelves. My parents were avid readers and both my parents have authored many books. Growing up, I did not share the love for reading that I feel now. I guess it took time and maturity to understand the power that lay within the pages. I am grateful to my parents for planting the seeds that translated into the courage to write my first book.*

*Obrigada Papi e Mami*

## FOREWORD

The premature burial of the human spirit (before actual death) is one of the most distressing things to encounter face to face! How could a person be this hurt and tragically broken? So broken, in fact that they replace their hope and love of life with hopelessness and despair and say, "God Must Hate Me." Sound familiar?

Miriam Grunhaus and I have something in common, this was our story... a shared story from two different worlds and two different perspectives. The profound fact, it could be your story too. Have you ever been broken? Have you ever tried to put the pieces back together of your shattered life? Everybody has a story, and this is one story that's so profoundly impactful because it's Real as Rain.

You are not a victim or a survivor! You were born to thrive. When you finish the amazing manuscript of one brilliant woman scarred by a lost dream, trying to "figure out" a way out through the fire that became her life. Screaming "why... why me...why God?" You will never think about seashells, vases, Kintsugi, scars, sparkling, small steps, messes, grief, gaps, gold and self-talk quite the same as you did before. Reading this work, pinned with the pain of knowledge that you were broken but not defeated. It is never too late to mend and construct a better you with the gold of the master. You were destined to be great. You are someone special.

My mother, Shirley Cummings was the most brilliant person I ever met. She would have loved Miriam. She would have loved her energy, her enthusiasm and zest for life. My Mother said many times: "Nothing like a woman scarred that lives to talk about it." What a difference they will make with all the scars in hand, bathed by adversity of their pain, tendered by the sadness only to come out victorious standing tall for all the world to see. Humbled, gracious and strong. When life happens to you, how will you respond? To quote my Mother, "Life is difficult but then it gets better if you choose to look up and believe". Thanks Mom.

I think God had his hand on the pen as Miriam wrote this manuscript. He gave her the special insight required to understand the women she interviewed. To get inside the women's pain to really listen and to develop a deep level of understanding. In some ways she wrote their story beautifully and eloquently and with stories that touched the soul with inspiration. You will "feel something" when you read this book. You will ask empowering questions. You will laugh and you will cry and be emotionally transported to someplace unique where you can take a good hard look at your life. Are you ready to go on this amazing journey?

I was a speaker, a teacher and an author. I take books very seriously. My Grandfather told me to "Drink from good books until you are intoxicated by wisdom." I love a Good Book. I have 5300 in my library and keep notes in every book. My favorite books I keep in a very special shelf that I like to call "Wisdom for The Ages". This is going in that special place. When I read the book, I was struck by the pain in the pen. I was intrigued by Miriam zest for life. Her father used to describe her to his friends as "The one with so much Joie de Vivre!" Miriam you have earned it by picking yourself up, gathering the broken pieces and taking the time to practice Kintsugi on your own life. You have written a masterpiece to be treasured.

I had an ischemic stroke May 13, 2018 on Mother's Day. I was unable to say a word, read or write. The doctors said I would never be able to communicate again. I am living proof if you pick up the shattered pieces of your torn-up life... you can with patience put it back together stronger than it was before. Let go and let God. After all you not being demolished you are being polished with gold.

**Paul Cummings**
Founder
PaulCummings WorldWide
Woople
Tech Town
The Level 10 Campus
Author of "It All Matters"

Miriam Grunhaus

*Author, Speaker, Fashion Designer, Marketer*
*#IamKintsugi*
*Miriam is native of Brazil, she lives with her family in Florida*
*To reach the author, email: info@healwithgold.com*

## NOTE TO READER

## The best way out is always through – Robert Frost

You know when life punches you in the gut so hard that you are literally brought down to your knees, trying to breathe? You know how when someone sees you in pain their first reaction is to touch your back and ask you "Are you okay?"

"Nope, not okay and please don't touch me. I need to use every ounce of strength to breathe and stay alive right now!"

You need to be left alone and pray that you can survive the next minute.

Life had brought me to my knees. I always loved life and I was not prepared to let my circumstances get in my way of living fully and joyfully. My father used to describe me to his friends as "The one with so much Joie de Vivre!" (Zest for life) I couldn't have him be wrong, I was proud that he admired how simple things brought me so much happiness and fulfillment.

In our living room, my husband and I sat across from each other planted on the couches with hot tears streaming down our faces; so hot, they burned. We could barely move.

Out of the depths of my soul a voice came out and spoke to me. I looked up at my husband and said, "Let's go for a walk on the beach." As we arrived, I told him that we should look for shells, put the pain we felt onto those shells, and throw them into the ocean, like a ritual to see if we could get some relief from our pain.

We walked in silence, gathering as many shells as we could find. Then, putting the shells up to our lips we very quietly said, "You are the pain I feel for all the disappointments in my life. To the next shell, "You are the pain I feel for being misunderstood, no matter how much I try to explain myself." Third shell, "You are all the pain from all the abuse we felt." Fourth shell, "You are the pain for my shattered dreams." Fifth shell, "You are the pain I feel toward those who were supposed to stand up for me and protect me but didn't." There were so many shells we tossed into the ocean to carry away our pain.

As we walked in the soggy sand where the tide barely touched our toes, I turned to my husband and said, "We asked God for solutions. We asked God for guidance. We asked God to take this pain away... but we did not ask God to help us survive this and go through it with less difficulty."

We thought we knew what we needed to have happen, and we asked for those specific results, but maybe what we want is not the best for us, and what we need to go through, despite it being hard and painful, is necessary and has a valid reason that is hidden from us. We need God by our side, supporting us through this time of growth. We need to ask Him to hold us and help us through these growing pains and we must believe that we need to go through this and not around of this.

So, we did just that. We asked for help and love and support. We asked God to not forsake us.

We received a personal and immediate miracle, and we felt better. We felt stronger, less alone. It was as if God said, "Finally you two figured out what you had to ask…"

Empowered to survive, knowing that we didn't need all the solutions, and we didn't need to understand why, but we needed to believe that it was for a greater good and that we are deeply loved, regardless of the pain we felt. We realized at that moment, that together we would survive, and hopefully one day soon, we would feel joy again.

This book is a combination of my thoughts through the journey from victim to survivor to thriver, where I share the lessons I learned from the very strong, resilient women I interviewed, and the lessons I learned from the Japanese art of Kintsugi, that showed me, visually and through its philosophy, that everything is mendable, and always better once mended with gold. I am so happy you are here!

#WEAREKINTSUGI

# TABLE OF CONTENTS

| | |
|---|---|
| FORWORD | I |
| NOTE TO READER | V |
| ONE When A Heart Breaks | 23 |
| TWO Kintsugi And All Its Glory | 29 |
| THREE The Dream - The Kintsugi Tribe | 37 |
| FOUR Victim, Survivor, Thriver, Which One Are You? | 49 |
| FIVE What Does Kintsugi Have To Do With Healing? | 59 |
| SIX Golden Nugget #1 - Taking Responsibility | 77 |
| SEVEN Golden Nugget #2 - Belief In A Higher Power | 85 |
| EIGHT Golden Nugget #3 - The Power Of Patience | 93 |
| NINE Golden Nugget #4 - Living With Intention | 107 |
| TEN Golden Nugget #5 - We Are Better Together | 121 |
| ELEVEN Golden Nugget #6 - Vantage Points | 131 |
| TWELVE Golden Nugget #7 - Letting Go | 141 |
| THIRTEEN Golden Nugget #8 - Attitude Of Gratitude | 151 |
| FOURTEEN Golden Nugget #9 - Self-Kindness | 159 |
| FIFTEEN Golden Nugget #10 - Acts Of Kindness | 169 |
| SIXTEEN Rewrite Your Next Chapter | 181 |
| ACKNOWLEDGMENTS | 189 |
| IN MEMORIAM | 193 |
| ENDNOTES | 195 |
| BOOK CLUB QUESTIONS | 199 |

## CHAPTER ONE
## WHEN A HEART BREAKS

Sometimes good things fall apart so better things can fall together. - *Marilyn Monroe*

It is interesting how we have a vision of ourselves and our future. Often, we think we know what we are here on Earth to do; other times we don't, but we do recognize strengths and attach our purpose to those strengths. We also have predetermined thoughts about the "right" thing to do and be, and what is honorable. If we believe in these qualities and behaviors, we think we need to do them and be them.

But when life steers us in a different direction, it can come as a blow. The fact that we imagined our life a certain way and have expectations of the results we will get from living that way, and they don't happen as we predicted or expected, is itself a hardship we must overcome.

### EXPECTATIONS

In a way, expectations are so closely connected to dreams and goals that they are generally what moves us forward in a growing trajectory. Unfulfilled expectations leave people disappointed, sad, broken, and feeling inadequate.

My life's expectations were that I would work hard and succeed. I would build a beautiful family and we would all love each other and thrive together. I would raise my family to be strong and independent.

My husband and I would have the most harmonious marriage and we would grow old together, travel the world, and share many wonderful experiences. We would be healthy, in good shape, I would continue being relatively thin as I was growing up. I would remain active and joyful.

Small wins would be reasons for great celebration. I would work in the creative field and share my constantly flowing ideas with the world. My business would grow, I would have employees doing the work I didn't much like, and I would be immersed in all that I loved.

When our children arrived, I would teach them the values of ethics and integrity that I had learned from my parents, so that they, too, would thrive and prosper. I expected to enjoy the grandkids when they came along, spoiling them as I should, and watching them growing happily.

Then there were all the dreams that I conjured in my youth at that time when you are in the zone, free to drift into ecstasy. In those dreams I would run long marathons, I would join a covert unit that saves the world and destroys terrorists, and I would save little children from doomsday. At one point, I thought my calling and mission for my time on this planet was to open an orphanage. I did not know how I would make what I thought was my purpose a reality, but these dreams brought me joy and kept me excited about all my possibilities.

A line is a compilation of little dots all so close to each other that they look like one continuous shape. Just like how life is: a bunch of little bumps close to one another forming our day-to-day. In between the dots is the space where we will be tested, and our character will be built.

I am a visual person and I think the easiest way to describe myself is as a vase filled with beautiful vibrant flowers, each representing my family members. My purpose was to be the vessel to contain the water that would sustain my family. I felt I was supposed to keep them close to each other, to support them and create an environment where they could flourish, adorn the world, making God, my family, and myself proud.

THEN LIFE HAPPENED.

It was as if my vase fell to the ground and shattered into a million little pieces. Some shards were so small that they might as well have been sand. The vase was no longer a tangible piece of pottery. My self-worth was shattered, my reason for being no longer existed, and I just did not know how to proceed. I didn't know how to move to the next chapter when the current chapter of my life was so completely different than my visions and expectations.

Since my story is not only mine, and out of respect for all involved, I will not spend too much time in its details. Frankly the details don't really matter or change the big picture. I learned that from all the women I have interviewed. The path to Joy doesn't change by the adversity experienced but rather by our reactions to it.

I can share with you that our family broke apart, and I experienced, what I call a loss of the living. Being that all were alive and well, I did not even know how to grieve. I was shocked. I was falling fast into a deep dark vortex of pain and hurt. I have learned that this type of grief is experienced by people who are disconnected from their loved ones by any number of reasons like illness, addiction, politics and others.

My grief spiraled into many other losses as those around me did not meet my expectations of supporting me emotionally. They did not rescue me or help resolve the situation and in some instances made it worse.

My family was torn apart. Misunderstandings turned into painful words, disagreements, fights, and finally distance and disconnect. I was the one who was supposed to keep us together, happy and flourishing, and I alone had failed at my self-appointed purpose.

Like the vase, I was shattered and believed that I would stay sad and broken forever. The failure, the sadness, the anger, the despair, the loneliness was deep, palpable and I didn't know how to fix it. I sincerely thought that this was it. I would not rebound this time, because there was no way to put that vase back together. There was no healing, no mending, and no hope.

I felt that losing a living loved one was worse than death. There was no closure, there was a living soul, one that I loved more than life, that was continuing their journey and I was not a part of it, I was not welcome. I had failed. I was a failure. I had a simple job and I couldn't complete it.

As I was going through my family ordeal a neighbor lost her 12-year-old daughter to a skateboarding accident. I thought about how that mother would never laugh again, smile again, feel joy again. I made a judgment about myself and about others. I really believe that when you are in the darkest of places you cannot see the light, not even a flicker.

I was seeing despair everywhere. My brain was creating a stream filled with sadness. I was feeling more and more depressed. I did not believe I could ever heal.

Like many women, I am the caretaker of my family. I am the one who fixes everything and I set out to repair this rift. I set myself up to solve, explain, and talk to people who were more qualified and more spiritual than me, but I was not managing to resolve the discord and reduce the distance. I was not fixing anything. This time it seemed that my desire to fix was creating more issues.

It was that walk on the beach with my husband that finally made me understand that I could not fix this problem. I understood the only way to resolve the pain was to experience it. Until that day I did not know that the point of grieving was really to feel and to go through and not around my circumstances.

I felt defeated. At the same time, once I accepted that I was not in control and I could not fix the problem and really, all I was able to do was lean in, I felt that I had a "job," a purpose, and a reason for being. And right during that time of my life, the purpose was to feel and live the pain and not to fight it. I needed to believe in the process.

I still felt broken, a shattered mess. Days passed, weeks passed, and I wanted to mask and numb the pain. I had to find something to distract me, something that would keep me sane, alive, and productive. So, I started a new business, a fashion brand, working almost 18 hours a day. While immersed in the creativity and the demands of building my brand I could barely feel the pain that had a choke-hold around my heart. The rest of the time was hard. Until something happened that would change the trajectory of my life forever.

CHAPTER TWO

# KINTSUGI AND ALL ITS GLORY

There is a saying in Tibetan, 'Tragedy should be utilized as a source of strength.' No matter what sort of difficulties, how painful experience is, if we lose our hope, that's our real disaster. — *The 14th Dalai Lama*

Sitting on my bed on a Sunday afternoon pondering my life and my new business, I received a WhatsApp message with a video from a friend. Frankly, I hadn't heard from him in a while and deep down I was resentful. I felt he hadn't been there for me during my time of pain.

I decided to watch the video and it was more than just a "thinking of you" message, it changed my life. That video planted a seed in my brain that gave me a purpose, some direction, and hope.

KINTSUGI

In the video, Sean Buranahiran[1] explains the art of Kintsugi and how it relates to human beings. The Japanese art of Kintsugi is the art that mends pottery with lacquer and gold, the gold highlights the breaks, it is not meant to fix in a way that hides where the pottery had been broken; rather, it emphasizes the breaks.

As art, a pottery that is fixed in Kintsugi becomes more expensive, more valuable for the gold, and for the time and artistry that it took to fix it. The piece becomes more beautiful, unique and stronger than before it broke.

As a philosophy, Kintsugi teaches us so many lessons. To begin with, everything can be fixed and mended. It shows that just like the mended Kintsugi pottery we also become more valuable, unique, and strong.

The art is time-consuming and requires much skill, patience, vision, and commitment. The art celebrates imperfection, it teaches us to be proud of our scars as opposed to being embarrassed by them. By highlighting the breaks, it demonstrates how those breaks are actually what is interesting and special about us, not something to be ashamed of, or that should be hidden.

When a piece of the broken pottery is lost, it can be filled with gold or with another fragment from a different piece of pottery, even if it doesn't match. It is not about blending and hiding; rather, it is about highlighting. It visually shows, to the visual learners like me, that when we break and even when parts are broken to dust, we can always be repaired, and there is always hope.

That video filled me with hope, and I became curious about, even a bit obsessed with Kintsugi, I needed to learn more about the art, how and why it was conceptualized and developed. So many inventions happen by accident and I needed to know more. I started consuming everything I could find on the subject.

Most importantly, I realized that just as a broken vase could be put back together, and it would look differently than before, I could, too. And I did not need to feel shame. If I did the work required, I would be more valuable with wisdom and empathy, with strengths that I didn't possess until that point in my life. It was up to me to pick up the pieces and do the labor of a Kintsugi master. No one was coming to do the work for me. I now had a vision of what was possible. We are all the Kintsugi masters of our own lives. I felt an urgency to get to work.

### BETTER THAN BEFORE

In reading about Kintsugi I learned about the technical part and the philosophy behind the art. Historians believe that the art of Kintsugi dates back to the late 15th century. According to the legend, the craft was discovered when the Japanese shogun, Ashikaga Yoshimasa, sent his favorite tea bowl that had been cracked to China for repair. Yoshimasa was not happy with the metal staples used to put the pieces together.

Local Japanese craftsmen were motivated to help the shogun and one presented the Kintsugi method. The shogun loved his teapot even more once it was fixed and by the 17th century, Kintsugi became common practice. The Japanese philosophy of Wabi-Sabi calls for seeing beauty in the flawed or imperfect and Kintsugi is very much a part of the Wabi-Sabi way of living.

The Kintsugi process is time-consuming. The mending, drying, perfecting, and dusting are all very laborious and have to be done just so, for the pieces to mesh together and remain strong and stable. When complete the piece becomes stronger, especially in the areas where it had been broken before.

Kintsugi is not just about salvaging pottery. It is a lesson for life; it is hope for the living. The Japanese are very respectful of their elders. They see them as the source of knowledge and luck. They keep their elders near them, present in their business because they believe it brings luck, and they also bring wisdom. They see the time, the wrinkles, and the breaks as the uniqueness that they gathered through living, through experiencing, as good influence. Elders are revered and honored.

Kintsugi teaches us that we are not to be discarded if we break, we are not trash or waste; rather, we are worth the time and attention to fix, because once fixed and mended we are way more valuable than before. Living is the process of Kintsugi, because the point of living is to become better versions of ourselves, to grow in value, and strengthen our character.

The process of Kintsugi is hard; as is the process of mending broken hearts and mending broken lives. But we, like Kintsugi pottery, are worth the time and effort to be mended and fixed.

At times in our lives, we go through incredible hardships and pain. We think that we are not worthy, and we can't afford the time and effort to fix ourselves, and at times we feel it is too late or that we are not capable of making things better. But it is never too late to devote the time and attention to perfect ourselves.

After we do the work and are mended and healed, we are way more valuable than before. Imagine a $5 treasured ceramic can be worth hundreds or even thousands of dollars after it is fixed, depending on how many breaks needed mending. The wisdom we gain from our experiences is what makes us more unique and special. It is really the reason for all of us being on this planet.

For those of us who are parents, it is clear how we love our kids with all our might. No matter how imperfect they are, no matter how many mistakes they may have made, no matter how many times they misbehaved or did not follow our directions or requests, no matter how annoying or infantile they may be, no matter if they broke our favorite dish... nothing comes close to the love we feel for these beings. Your child has done nothing to earn this love. You just love them because they just "are," and because they are yours.

We are all children of our Creator. Do you think that we were brought into this world to then be forsaken? I don't believe that for a second. I believe wholeheartedly that the love is deep and unbreakable. That the love is unconditional, that we were given the possibility to choose, and even if we choose poorly, we are still loved.

I actually dare to say that I would not be surprised if our Creator is offended by how we belittle ourselves and say that we are not worth the work, that we are not worth love. Why would God impose these hardships on us? Why do good people have to suffer? These questions are hard for us to answer with the limited wisdom we have. But think of it this way...

When our kids misbehave, we punish them. We totally understand that it is for their own good. But do they understand that? Do they think that we are the honorable and courageous parent? That we are all knowing and wise and that whatever we do for them is the right course of action? I don't think so, I think they are angry at us and don't understand why we would cause them pain if we indeed love them.

It is all about perspective. In this world we are the children of our Creator and at times the lessons we must learn are terribly painful. Just like a teenager who loses their phone for bad grades, we can't see the Gestalt, we can't see the big picture, and we can't see what is really good for us. We can only see what we see with our human eyes.

The fact that we don't see or understand doesn't make it less painful or less hard. It is why belief and trust in a higher power is so helpful. When you have that blind faith, you understand that it is hard; you know that it is painful, but you also know that there is love and there is a good reason for the trajectory we are going through. One that we are out to discover but at times will never fully understand.

When I was in art school, a professor taught us how to build with clay. We worked the entire semester on our pieces. Methodically perfecting our shapes, I was much better working in 2D than 3D, so for me it was an effort; and in the process, we were falling in love with our masterpieces. My classmates and I were commercial art majors; we were learning graphic design, illustration, advertising and the like. When we were all done creating and building our pieces, our professor broke every last one of them. We looked at the broken pieces and couldn't believe our eyes. There was silence.

Our professor then explained to us that we were not fine

artists, we were commercial artists. We were not creating for our own egos, for our own likings, we were not creating so we could display our creations and receive accolades. We were creating so that our clients could prosper; so they would ultimately get the most ROI (Return on Investment), as our function was to sell products and services and not create something beautiful.

We would need to learn to disconnect ourselves from our art, listen closely to our clients, do what they wanted us to do, and at times butcher our work because they want to add huge red arrows in the middle of the design to bring attention and ultimately sell their product. Our professor made it clear: we would be serving our employers, not ourselves. We were providing a service, not creating something to serve our needs and desires. She gave us all A's, but she gave us much more than that. She gave us a lesson in perspective, which in itself was worth four years of private college tuition.

We are here for a reason, and not just to enjoy, have fun at the beach, travel, earn, spend, and then disappear. That is not why we were bestowed the privilege to live in this amazingly beautiful and magical world. We came for a purpose and to achieve knowledge so we can fulfill our need to be molded and learn and grow... and the path to that is long and hard and the journey, at times, is very painful. I fully believe that when you understand that, you accept the hardships with a completely different perspective.

If we were talking about physical fitness it is easy to understand that it is an ongoing process. The work is continuous, and it is hard, and includes denying yourself certain pleasures of the world. But those who are careful with what they eat and how they exercise, do that because they know and fully understand the benefit of their hard work, not because it is easy.

Life is a gym; the most important gym of all times. The one that will shape us from inside, mold us, and strengthen us so we can use our strengths in this world to do good things, to build and not break, to help and to serve, to leave this planet a better place than we found it. If we don't, we will have missed the point.

While in this gym we will have to carry some heavy loads, it will hurt, we will need to fall and rise and fall and rise many times, we will have to part with some people we love, whether they are leaving this world or maybe just because they are not meant to be part of our journey. We will feel some physical pain, which will alert us to issues we need to resolve, and the list is really long, but all of it is in preparation for us to become one of the most beautiful Kintsugi pieces ever created.

Scars are signs that we survived these tests, trials, and tribulations. But golden scars are the signs that we thrived after we survived. It means that we are now richer in wisdom; we are more unique and well rounded. We are more empathetic, we are givers, healers, helpers and we are actively working toward making this planet a better place… even if it is one person at a time, one woman at a time, one child at a time.

Whatever your journey leads you to be, and what you become, I can assure you that your mess will become your message if you relinquish the victim mentality and see the potential of what you can attain with your "gold."

## CHAPTER THREE
## THE DREAM – THE KINTSUGI TRIBE

*The whole secret of a successful life is to find out what is one's destiny to do, and then do it.* – Henry Ford

Seeing the Kintsugi art in that video was a transformational moment in my life. Looking at the pictures of the women painted with the gold lines going through them made it very concrete for me. I needed the visual to see the possibilities; I needed his soothing voice to make me believe.

I got the message. The message did not come in a bottle or some mystical source, it came via WhatsApp. We must be accepting and open-minded to receive the messages destined for us.

At that time, I was completely broken, shattered, and occasionally frozen in place. I did not believe that I would be able to heal. Throughout my life I had gone through many ups and downs and endured tests that were hard, and I was always strong enough to pull through. But I was not equipped to grieve a loss of the living. I couldn't deal with the fact that someone who I believed would always be part of my life, whom I loved so completely, didn't want to be part of it. How do you grieve such a loss without closure?

I wanted to speak to someone who would not judge me, and would understand how broken I was feeling, I needed to speak to someone who was positive, who had strong energy, and had faith. I called Aliza. Her personal story is one of many ups and downs. She has lived through many tragedies and her faith is unscathed. Her wisdom is ever illuminating, and I love her dearly. I shared with Aliza that I felt that I was being punished and that I felt unloved. Her words brought me much comfort.

## THE MATRIARCHS

Aliza mentioned the mothers in the Bible, the matriarchs; Sara, Rebecca, Rachel, and Leah. She asked me if I thought God loved them. I replied that yes, I thought God loved them for their wisdom, their faith, and their piousness. Aliza went on to share how much they suffered in their lives with infertility, moving from place to place; how Rachel gave the love of her life to her sister without knowing if he, Jacob, would work for her father for another seven years to marry her as well. These are stories I knew well but didn't consider while dealing with my pain.

Aliza asked me to imagine how they felt having to send their "bad" sons away, sons that maybe were not so great, but were their sons. They suffered, they had pain, and they were loved. They were also the most special role models. If they suffered, why did I think I was above them to live life without any major ordeals? And maybe God loved me as He loved them because God was testing me with an adversity of similar proportions.

One of our conversations shifted my perspective from victim (poor me... no one loves me not even God), to: could it be that I have such high potential to repair and become a role model myself? That my pain would have purpose and this purpose would help many?

I fully realized that I could put my pieces together, in theory. I also understood that I am loved, that I have great potential, and that I have what it takes to do the work to fix my life, and maybe the Kintsugi gold I would add would, in essence, be my new purpose in life.

I reasoned it this way: I am the ceramic. I am that vase I thought broken beyond repair. I believed I could never put my pieces together, but God (universe or whatever you believe in) brought this video to my attention to show me visually that it is not true. That everything can be mended and if done properly, carefully, and thoughtfully it can be more valuable than before.

Finally, I was committed. I became determined to learn how to put my pieces back together. I understood the time I will need to sit in my pain. I understood the filing of the ceramics that is needed before gluing the pieces together. I understood that some pieces broke into sand and I will need to fill them in with either a different piece or with a lot of gold... I understood that it will take polishing to make it all even and smooth, but what is the Gold? What is that special gift that is added that will make me more unique, stronger, more valuable, more desired, more than I was before? I did not know; I did not have the answers and so I began my search for the gold.

During the period of my life when I went through my adversity, I was working in my boutique graphics and marketing firm. Through the years I built an amazing clientele, mostly major pharmaceutical companies that paid me to do what I loved: teach employees and implement programs that promoted ethics and compliance. I was raised by parents whose integrity was unquestionable. My father was a man with ethics and integrity that were admired by all who met him and working in this field not only gave me pleasure and satisfaction, it also gave my father great pride. I loved that I was honoring my parents' lessons of deciphering right from wrong and leading a life of honesty and integrity, and I was fully immersed in what I valued - all submerged in creativity, as I had to find ways to promote and market such a dry and theoretical subject.

My heartbreak hit at the same time that my business suffered a decline, mostly due to mergers and acquisitions in the Pharma world. Everything was happening at the same time. I didn't see it then but looking back, it was a blessing. Frequently you will notice the pattern of blessings after you've overcome hardships.

At the time, I felt ready to start something new and I used the act of working as my drug of choice. I wanted to change my business because I wanted to do something I knew nothing about. I knew I could learn; I am smart and resourceful; I knew I would get good at it because I was always very determined. I knew I had what it took, and mostly it was time. I would fill every waking moment with learning, growing and building because every moment I did that, I did not think of my pain, my loss, my situation, my shame, my embarrassment, and my vulnerability. I always thrived when I was creating, innovating and doing.

But I know very well that the intensity of that devotion was nothing more than a way to run away and numb the pain. It is okay to give a name to our actions and recognize the reasons, so we learn for the future.

To bury my pain, I opened my fashion company Mikah Fashion (www.MikahFashion.com). At first, I designed handbags, traveling to Italy, buying the most beautiful leathers, crafting bags, importing bags, and selling to small specialty boutiques. I had to learn about leather quality, manufacturing, importing, exporting, duties, shippers, trade shows, how to handle the accounts, selling online, and for the first time I had to deal with B2C (business to consumer), as my expertise had always been B2B (business to business).

## THE SHARK

Saying that I was busy is a gross understatement. Within my first year I was in boutiques nationwide, my site was up after we had incorporated, and I had a business. But I realized very quickly that it would take millions to make this a successful brand. Millions I did not have. So, I decided to test the clothing business and manufactured one style to see how it did. It sold well and rather fast. I wanted to brainstorm what to do so I decided to ask for help, but not help as in money. I requested the opinion of a "shark." I have a friend who happens to be extremely successful in business. Think of Mr. Wonderful from Shark Tank, on steroids. I asked him if he would grant me a favor and come to my office for a conversation. I showed him my showroom and I shared the status of my business.

These were his first words:

*"Miriam, are you a moron?"*

I answered… *"I don't think I am, but I may indeed be…. Tell me what I am doing wrong."*

His answer was: *"Drop the bags. Don't even spend another minute liquidating them – just continue with the clothing."*

My bags were retailing for about the same as a "Coach" bag because of the high cost of manufacturing and importing them from Italy, but if a woman had to choose between buying a brand name plastic bag or an Italian leather bag with no recognizable brand, she would go for the branded bag because she was not buying a bag, she was buying the status that came with the branded bag. So, I started doing dresses as a test and created styles that were selling well.

When my friend saw that the dresses were doing well, he wanted me to focus on that. He also thought I had too many SKUS (stock-keeping units). He was right. He was right about the SKUS, he was right about the dresses, and he was right that I was a moron, at least in that area of my business.

Most people will say he could have kept that part to himself, but as I have mentioned, I am strong, and I accepted the constructive criticism. In fact, I felt honored that he wanted to help me and give me the gift of the truth. Trust me, it is a gift. Most don't share that honesty and if you can handle it, you will get redirected when you make a mistake and it will save a lot of aggravation, time, and money.

Mikah became a clothing brand. After two years of hard work, our clothing line was being sold in about 40 boutiques nationwide and even some internationally, but I was not happy. I was looking at my clothing line and feeling disconnected. I would not even consider myself a true fashionista. I would much prefer to put on my jogging suit, so I could sit comfortably at my desk all day or jeans overalls (much more my personal casual, earthy style); remember...I was still in hiding. I was still drugging myself with work, numbing myself from my pain. But numbing or not, I am also an entrepreneur at heart, and I was building a business. I just needed to find the heart of it so I could actually be proud of what I was creating.

## MY WHY

In Simon Sinek's book, *Start With Why*, he explains that people won't truly buy into a product, service, movement, or idea until they understand the WHY behind it and I needed to know my personal Why for choosing to work in fashion when I personally don't feel super connected to the fashion world. I was also very influenced by the book, *A Story Brand*, by Donald Miller. If you have a business, I highly recommend reading it. In Miller's book he explains how people don't buy products; they buy experiences, they buy stories, and I needed to figure out my why and my story, ultimately my brand's story.

I received the Kintsugi video about the same time this feeling of lack of personal satisfaction from the business was sinking in, so when I had an "Aha!" moment for my personal life, that also changed the business. I literally jumped off that bed after I watched the video. I had just found out I could put my pieces together and I would be okay, my life would be okay. But I also found out my why! I didn't care about clothing, per se. I cared about the women who I was serving. I wanted to connect with them at a deeper level. I wanted to take them through my healing journey and ultimately help them heal as well.

IDEAS

I have many and frequent ideas. I describe my brain as "sparkling" or like it's a bunch of "firecrackers." After seeing the video and immersing myself in Kintsugi, I had the idea to change my clothing line into a Kintsugi-inspired collection so that I could share the message that saved my soul. I wanted all women to know that we can all heal, that we are worth the work, that we are all beautiful in our imperfections, that no one has a how-to manual for life, so we all make mistakes and we are not less special because of it. There is always a way to rebuild.

I designed a clothing line and four months later it was displayed at South Florida International Fashion Week (SFIFW) show. My new life had begun. It would be the life where I was going to put my pieces together, while I was connecting with other women who also wanted to put their pieces together. I started the journey of learning and sharing, rinsing and repeating. The hashtag #WeAreKintsugi was born. I wanted to share with people that we are all worth the fixing. We all have a story. We all have our messes that become our messages and we don't have to be ashamed of our history. Instead, we should be proud, as we are better because of it.

CURIOSITY MADE ME DO IT...

I wanted to find out what differentiated the women who went through hardship and thrived, from those who stayed victimized by their circumstances, many of them leading a life of destruction. I knew some women were naturally strong, as I felt I was too, but I felt it was impossible that all women who went through adversity and considered themselves joyful were all naturally strong. I knew many had done hard work to achieve the lifestyle and joy they were feeling. I set out to find and interview them, learn what they had gone through, and how they healed. I wanted to know what it took.

I believe wholeheartedly that God blessed me with the Kintsugi video, and now He blessed me with the connections to the right women who were about to share with me their journeys.

I began interviewing women regularly for almost two years as of the writing of this book. I learned that many of them worked very hard at their healing journey and even though some attained it rather fast for others it took five or 10 plus years to heal. I also learned that they were not all born strong, but they exhibited strength in that they did not want to be victims of their circumstances.

I learned that no matter the age, background, ethnicity, religion, and a person's looks, the journey to healing took a familiar path. That is why I don't believe that the details of my story or anyone's story for that matter are crucial to understanding how you can heal. The most important part is what we can take from these stories to make our lives more whole and more joyful. We tend to put people in categories. But the biggest discovery was that the adversity didn't matter. The journey to healing was very similar. That blew my mind!

I realized that these women who came from completely different backgrounds, who were not naturally resilient, and yet could all achieve joy, could all heal, by doing the same basic things. That became the driving force to push me forward to write this book, to create a healing course, and to continue speaking about this to anyone who would want to listen.

We say that we were not given a manual to life, that each situation is completely different, and we all end up making our own mistakes, but in reality we do have a manual to healing and if we could all implement it, we could all experience a more joyful life.

The next chapters will uncover some of the most important actions taken by these women, which if implemented correctly, if done continuously, even when you don't get instant joy, will bring you closer to your personal healing.

I TRIED IT AND IT WORKED.

One day I woke up feeling lighter, feeling the pain and acknowledging the pain, but also sensing the blessings hidden in my trajectory. I knew that there was a reason, bigger than myself, that I had to be of service, that I had to be of value, that I could help others. But we can't be the "vase" and we can't be givers, and we can't keep doing for others, until we first put ourselves back together. First, we must introspect and clean up our messes.

**My mess became my message. My beautiful new vase became a symbol of what is possible for me and for others.**

I believe that within us we all have what I call a "joy-o-meter." We can measure how much joy we feel, and how long it lasts. But in order to get a good measure, we have to be very honest. We have to tell the truth. I think that we all feel tremendous joy when we feel good, look good and do things that give us instant reward. However, these joyous moments, the things we acquire, are not the type of joy that lasts.

And the more I realized and introspected about the recording of my joy-o-meter, the less I gave importance to the things I once felt were important in my life. My needs and desires changed, so did my priorities and I become a joy junkie. I wanted to feel it, I wanted to fill my life with it, and I was ready to do the work, take the responsibility, and begin that journey. I also wanted to fill others with it. I wanted to shout from the rooftops that joy is attainable, even for those who suffered the worst of tragedies.

JOY IS NOT CONSTANT.

When you start the journey to joy, you will soon learn that this search is eternal, that you find it and at times you lose it and you just need to steer back onto the road that will lead you to the joyful moments that are meaningful and long-lasting.

For me, the more I helped women, the more I told their stories and treated them with love and kindness, the more they felt not judged and safe to share their stories because they wanted to help others, brought more joy to me. I really felt this was my purpose and the more I got close to my purpose, the more my joy-o-meter was showing me that I was getting closer to my reason for being. My life completely changed. It was no longer about my personal healing, but it was to be a voice for other women who had healed and the need to give hope to those who were still feeling distressed. It was to share some hope and a path to joy with those who were struggling.

Throughout this book I share snippets of stories that were gifted to me, so that others can hear and see that there is always hope, that you are always loved, and that there is no shame in your journey.

As Leonard Cohen said, *"There is a crack in everything, that is how the light gets in."*

CHAPTER FOUR

# VICTIM, SURVIVOR, THRIVER, WHICH ONE ARE YOU?

My mission in life is not merely to survive, but to thrive; and to do so with some passion, some compassion, some humor, and some style. – *Maya Angelou*

I embarked on a search to understand the women who had gone through adversity, yet considered themselves joyful. I wanted to know if there was something different about them that set them apart from the women who stayed stuck. I mostly wanted to know if their behaviors were similar and if it could be learned behaviors. I found out very quickly that there are stages we go through after hardship strikes. Some stay in the first or second stage, while others graduate to the third stage, which is where joy lives.

THE STAGES ARE: VICTIM – SURVIVOR – THRIVER

THE VICTIM

The victim is that person who feels cheated, is angry, and believes that life is unfair. Victims' messes are worse than most. They are, in essence, center-focused and consider themselves forgotten, unloved, misunderstood, and feel that they are not getting what they deserve. To them, life is unjust. They struggle with accountability and think that whatever they did does not equal how much they are suffering; the punishment is disproportionate to their responsibility. The victim feels that she is a good person, but deep inside, she secretly doubts that she is. Victims have a mixture of self-doubt and anger, with a dash of "life is not fair."

They question where God is if they come from a background of faith. They don't believe that there could be a higher power because a higher power would never cause such injustice. They feel abandoned by family and friends, and they don't understand or accept that their behaviors are causing them constant disconnect. They don't see their responsibility in their hardship; like the failure of a marriage, or business, or any type of relationship. If they suffer illnesses, infertility, or mental health, they feel that they got the short stick and because of that, people need to come toward them and care for them, be sensitive to them, and be understanding of their limitations.

The victim is sad and depressed, but also very angry and at times, impulsive. The victim can't stop thinking of the injustices and she harbors much anger, disdain, and animosity toward others who do not come to solve her problem or whose lives seem perfect. The victim can be jealous.

Victims ask the universe for a solution, and when the answer doesn't come, they feel validated in their thoughts that there is no one to help them; otherwise, their problems would have been solved.

Life becomes hard, and many don't see a reason for living. Days turn into months, moments of fleeting joy are rare, and it starts affecting every part of a victim's life, including her physical and emotional health, appearance, and relationships with others.

Most people don't want to be around someone who is negative and pessimistic and who likes to talk about how everyone else is at fault. Even if we feel that way sometimes, we don't want anyone else around us to be that downer. So, the victim starts losing her friends and one day she wakes up and realizes that she's a party of one on a very lonely island.

Many victims do a good job hiding their feelings and to strangers, they seem very cool and collected; however, these relationships never become deep because victims reserve their feelings to those close to them. Victims tend to make their own messes even messier.

*Are you a victim of your circumstances?*

We all go through periods of feeling victimized, as individuals and even as groups. While many of us manage to graduate to survivor, some stay stuck and are unable to live joyful, fulfilling lives.

## THE SURVIVOR

The survivor did a lot of work to overcome her situation. She left bad circumstances, she received treatment, she survived illnesses; she did the work, put in the time and felt very accomplished. She knows that she was in a very bad place and recognizes the improvement and how she succeeded to better her life. The survivor implemented better habits; she is protective of herself because she knows where she has been and where she came from. There is pride and relief. She remembers all too well the suffering and hardship she went through and she is relieved to be in a different situation.

The survivor is very cautious. She won't allow herself to go back into a place of danger, a place where she can fall back into old patterns; she is very attentive to her success.

The survivor is strong and resilient, but cautious, which leads her to a limited way of living.

Think of an artist, she takes that white canvas and goes to town, using almost all the colors on her palette, and feeling satisfied with her work. The painting looks beautiful, and it took a lot to get to that point. But it is unfinished. The survivor considers that maybe she should add more paint to continue her masterpiece and take it to the next level, but she is also afraid that if she does, she will ruin everything that she worked so hard for to get to this point. And so, she stops short. The fear of undoing, of taking chances, of feeling pain again

The main goal of the survivor is to learn techniques to live with what happened to her, but not necessarily learn or give purpose to the pain. She counts her blessings that she is able to breathe and function. Going to work is an accomplishment that makes her proud. She looks at every single action that she manages to do with pride, even though she remains fearful.

The survivor knows deep pain and her main focus is just as the name suggests: to survive. She goes through her days without getting into much trouble and manages her pain, anxiety, depression, and sadness. Good days are when she doesn't think of the hardship she has survived, and she gets many of them, due to much work and concentration. She feels like she has won, and she is satisfied; as she knows where she came from and stridently protects herself from going back

The survivor has the right to be proud of where she is right now. But the sweet spot of joy is right beyond the survivor stage and only some will actually survive AND thrive.

*Are you a survivor?*

## THE THRIVER

The women I interviewed and learned so much from are all Thrivers. The first thing they all have in common, and I found out rather quickly, is that all of them detest the concept of being a victim. They will not be described as such, they don't want to be pitied, and they don't want to stay in the pain for longer than they have to. They are willing to do the work and they are willing to take responsibility for whatever was in their control; they forgive themselves, they learn better, and they change.

From my research, even the naturally resilient women acknowledge that they were victims when the adversity happened, and they hated that feeling. They needed to get out of that place as fast as possible. The ones who were naturally resilient were able to take action to move them from victim to survivor. They immediately went into their personal toolbox (all survivors have them). They analyzed and they introspected, and they understood they needed time to grieve. They realized when they were sitting too long in the pain and that they should have done something sooner. They knew that now they needed to do more.

The Thriver needs to give purpose to her pain and she spends much time thinking about how to turn her misery into something better. The Thriver thinks about the bigger picture, how she can take her situation and use what broke her to help others. She knows that by helping others she is also empowering herself. She is naturally a giver and gets a lot of pleasure being of service and value to others. She wants to find the silver lining in her situation.

When you reach the Thriver stage, you feel stronger and are ready to find your purpose to move you through your pain. You are focused on being of service and helping others in similar situations. You feel that what you went through was for a good reason and you know you can help others in similar situations shorten their recovery time. You also possess a lot of knowledge, not only from experience, but because you really took time to learn about what happened to the women you are helping. By helping others, you will learn how they reacted and dealt with their pain brought on through similar situations.

A Thriver will do things out of her comfort zone to fulfill the needs of being of service and giving her pain a purpose. They become public speakers, write books, and share their stories openly. While survivors may feel shame or vulnerability, Thrivers are very aware that their sharing is healing for others and that momentary embarrassment is well worth it, if it will help others. That in itself brings them joy.

Thrivers keep flourishing from the energy of others who are inspired and empowered by their story. The encouragement they receive pushes them further to give more of themselves – to the point that sometimes the pain can become a blur because they have transformed into a different person. Thrivers wouldn't have wished to go through the adversity they experienced, but once they did, they saw their growth as a person, and felt their purpose. More importantly, Thrivers understand why they had to go through it. They don't resent it; they feel stronger and more empowered.

It takes time to become a Thriver, but the hours make you stronger. You will be hit by future adversities, because that is just how life is, but you will dig deep into your resilience toolbox, and remember that you are strong and able to get over the new struggles. You will also remember that you can always use the new experiences to help others. That thought is very motivating to a Thriver. The more she becomes comfortable with being a Thriver, the faster she bounces back from hardship. Becoming a Thriver is something that benefits her in all areas of her life. And that is why she is joyful.

Overcoming becomes wonderfully addictive. Thrivers want to overcome. They work hard to overcome, and they know very well from their own experience that they will gain a lot of joy and happiness from giving away their knowledge. Learning how to be a Thriver will ensure that throughout our lives we will bounce back from hardships in a faster and healthier way.

THRIVING

My personal journey has been difficult at times and I found myself being challenged by certain events that were sudden, difficult, and heartbreaking. None of it was easy and all of it made me stronger. As I write these words today, I am a better person from having experienced such adversity.

The fact that I have always been strong, independent, and resilient by nature was very helpful, but when I felt so broken, it took a lot of resilience tools to overcome the deep sadness I felt. Those resilience tools helped me go from Victim, to Survivor to Thriver; and this book is proof that sharing became my mission and my reason for being. I can tell you firsthand that when you feel that what you went through gives you the ability to help others, it will empower you and propel your mission to heal tenfold.

I learned from experience that we never arrive. It is not about the destination. It is about the journey and as such we can't wait for the light at the end of the tunnel. Now, I challenge you. Wouldn't you want to be the light to shine for others who are navigating in darkness? I would.

The interviews I have conducted with the women who felt joyful after they had faced adversity showed me that as long as a person is committed to the process and understands that it is going to be hard, she will take the time to heal and feel like a Thriver. This requires constant forward progress, which is more important than striving for perfection.

For each woman, the process began with small steps and a commitment to victory over their adversity. Thrivers feel it in their hearts that they will be successful. The next few chapters will describe parts of the process all the women I interviewed implemented and how they connect to the art of Kintsugi.

The art of Kintsugi is almost like a How-to-Heal map. The art teaches you that there is an order to the madness, it teaches specific things you need to focus on at each stage; it teaches you how to persevere because you can visualize the outcome. Most of all, it teaches you to understand what the Gold is.

CHAPTER FIVE

# WHAT DOES KINTSUGI HAVE TO DO WITH HEALING?

*Owning our story and loving ourselves through that process is the bravest thing that we will ever do.*
— Brené Brown

After seeing the Kintsugi video, my brain connected the dots. I saw "my vase" repaired, and I saw the beauty of the golden scars. In a very concrete way, I was able to imagine myself put back together and fully healed. I could also see that I would never look the same as my original self, and despite understanding the value of the original wholeness, there was a unique beauty in the scars. I had never quite appreciated that possibility before.

As I started learning more about the Kintsugi process and what it takes to create the repair, I was also able to put together the stages of healing. The same process for the art would be the process to heal my soul.

After learning the process of mending pottery, and conducting so many interviews with Thrivers, the connection between the art and healing a broken heart became clear. It was interesting to learn the importance of brokenness and the validity of having an "open heart" because ultimately, when the work is done properly, it is easier to see the importance of the break and the new space created. As Shannon Alder said, *"There is no perfection - only beautiful versions of brokenness."*

I share below the steps that every Kintsugi pottery goes through to become an amazing and unique piece of art, made whole and more beautiful than before. In doing so, the process connects us to our own healing, beginning with the same mindset as if mending a Kintsugi vessel.

# BROKENNESS

Close your eyes and imagine a beautiful vase sitting on the table. Suddenly, it slips from the table and crashes to the ground. As you look down, you see broken pieces splattered and scattered on the floor.

Most people sweep up the mess, hoping to get all the pieces of the vase so that no one unwittingly steps on a shard of glass. The vase is swept up and thrown in the trash. It was beautiful while it lasted; but now it is worthless.

Often times, we don't allow ourselves to properly grieve the loss of a broken art piece. We are quick to say, "It's just a vase, I can buy another, it is just a thing..." But we never allow ourselves to properly grieve for the loss of the piece. I am not talking about the vase you bought in Target that goes with the hall décor. I am talking about the vase you bought on your trip to Santa Fe or the vase you used for your wedding table 39 years ago. There could be many memories attached to that piece, but grieving is uncomfortable, and we are taught from an early age to wipe away our tears and move on. Unfortunately, we are doing a disservice by skipping the grieving process. Feeling is needed for a healthy recovery.

The Kintsugi philosophy teaches that grieving is very much a part of the process of healing and there is a value in sitting in the pain. When a bowl, dish, or vase breaks you must gather all the pieces and sit with them, then figure out if you found all the pieces. Did you get the tiny ones? Did you imagine the vase falling on the ground and where it was likely to scatter? You will know if you are missing pieces once you position all the bits together, like you would a puzzle. Are there areas missing a piece? Are the cracks thick or thin? Can you see what needs to be done to piece it back together again?

This process can be considered introspection, each piece representing events and time periods in our lives, giving us the time to reflect, reconcile, and renew. We ask ourselves about our expectations and dreams. How did they become undone? And what does it mean?

It is important to not only assess the situation, but to give it the time for proper grieving. It is uncomfortable, but it is necessary to remember and reminisce about the dreams undone, the disappointments, and the pain, we have to sit in it and allow ourselves to feel and not brush it away.

In the Jewish religion, there is a very descriptive way of how to mourn the loss of a person. You may have heard of the term that someone was paying a "Shiva call," which means to visit the mourner during the week after burial, where they sit at home on low chairs, mourning the loss of their loved ones.

There are very descriptive and specific laws on how a person needs to behave during the mourning period. There is value in grieving and there are many ways to grieve, depending on the circumstances. Also, in Jewish law, it teaches us when it is time to rejoice, and also how to transition from grieving to rejoicing. There is time to grieve and then there is time to rejoice and there are ways to do that, just as there are ways to put a pottery piece back together. Grieving is an important part of the journey but never a place we "move in full time."

While grieving is a necessary process of healing, it is temporary. We are not supposed to remain in misery. We are here to feel, learn, grow and evolve from the pains we suffer, the losses we experience, and the trauma we feel as victims. The pain comes with lessons that, if implemented, will surely strengthen your character and make you wiser and positively complex.

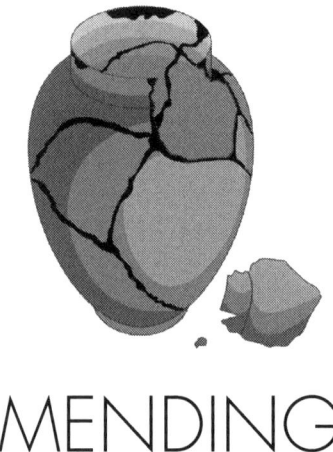

# MENDING

After finding the broken pieces, the Kintsugi master figures out where each piece should fit, just like a puzzle. The artist assesses if there are missing pieces and if so, how it will be filled in. Once that process is done, it is time for the mending to begin. The pieces are filed so their edges are smooth. The filing is necessary to ensure that the pieces will stick properly to each other and so they stay securely attached. The traditional glue used is called Urushi, it is a special lacquer that comes from Japanese trees.

In our own life, this is the time when we start implementing changes, like breaking our bad habits, and cutting it off with toxic people. Maybe we can also change the way we speak. We can commit to changing our behaviors and our environment for the better. But we must first decide what stays and what goes. Accept what has left, so that you can make a plan of action on how to "fill the gaps" and grow from your experiences and challenges.

In Kintsugi, at times it is necessary to fill gaps with pieces from other broken dishes in order to complete the original broken piece the Kintsugi master is working on. You will find that either parts were lost or pulverized upon impact and they cannot be recovered. The Kintsugi master may at times, fill these spaces with gold, which makes the piece even more valuable. Regardless of the decision on how to repair, the important part is to remember that there is always a way.

You must realize that you have multiple solutions to your adversity and different ways to deal with what has transpired. The biggest step is to accept that we will need to change and will no longer be the exact same person prior to the vase crashing to the floor.

The mending process requires bravery. Taking the first step shows courage. This introspection and assessment may be easier with the assistance of a third party for some, but I have also met many women who were able to do so by themselves, or with the assistance of some self-help books. Despite going through these changes by themselves without fail, the women who did it this way shared with me that they wished they had reached out for help because they could have expedited the process of healing. Maybe having a third party so we can speak out loud is a great way to hear ourselves and accept the guidance, knowing that it is a safe space and the person assisting is knowledgeable and non-judgmental.

Believing in our ability to succeed in overcoming our adversities is a crucial part of the healing process. The first mended pottery may not come out beautifully, and only if the Kintsugi artist continues the process and keeps at it, will she become a true master. And so, in life as well, it is imperative to believe that we can heal! But we will need determination and courage to keep mending, keep improving, and keep growing.

From my research the women who were ready to work on themselves and were successful had a sincere dislike of being pitied like some broken pottery shattered on the floor, dismissed as garbage. That dislike propelled them into action. They knew that when they succeeded in fixing what was broken, they would not be pitied. Rather, they would be admired for their incredible accomplishment in healing.

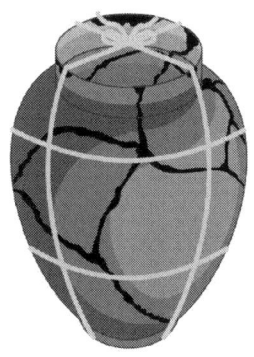

# CURING

The next step to creating your Kintsugi masterpiece is curing. After adding the Urushi lacquer and connecting the broken pieces, they need time to dry. It is important to tie a string around the piece to secure it; some masters put tape to hold the pieces together. The purpose of this step is to ensure that none of the pieces move, so that they dry perfectly in place. If the pieces move, they will not be "locked into place" to become the masterpiece you are trying to create.

THEN THE WAIT PERIOD BEGINS.

This, in my opinion, is one of the hardest parts of the process. At least it was for me. Understand that the wait time doesn't mean that you are not doing or creating; it is a sort of action through inaction. It is a time that your new behaviors transition into habits; they need to become part of the new you, so they don't dissolve and dissipate.

It is a time of reflection to figure out how to avoid similar situations in the future; learning from our mistakes is critical. We are making sure that the new friendships are genuine and toxic people are eliminated from our lives. During this time, repetition is vital to incorporate new habits and thought patterns, so each becomes part of the fabric that makes you who you are becoming. They need to become second-nature.

For those who are very active, whose brains are very "sparkling" like mine, this is a tough time. Stillness is not what I am known for, but I learned that it was necessary in order for me to keep going. The Thrivers I interviewed found the strength and a way to give themselves the time to construct their new behaviors, be kind to themselves, and learn how to become the new version of who they are meant to be.

Think of it this way. When we commit to changing the way we talk to ourselves, we have to remove stuff like "I am stupid" and "I am worthless." It will take a lot of time to change this bad habit and more importantly, this belief. Sometimes, the wait period is the longest. You may have heard the expression, "A watched pot never boils." It is like that; it requires tenacity and a deep wish to overcome and grow. We will keep falling back into old patterns, but if our desire to change is great, then we will re-direct ourselves onto the path of healing. Patience with the process and patience with ourselves and those around us may be difficult at times. Some may not believe in our healing, but we are committed to prove our determination.

As Mahatma Gandhi said: *"To lose patience is to lose the battle."* Just as an impatient Kintsugi master won't create the valuable art piece she strives to produce; we need to give the proper time to become who we are meant to be.

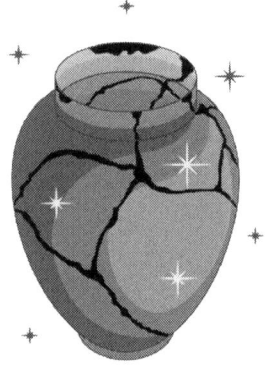

# POLISHING

So much work and time goes into a Kintsugi piece and it all leads to the most exciting part of all, this is when the master removes the tie or tape that has been around the piece, holding everything together. It is the moment of truth. Did the pieces stay put in their right places and can the master start the process of polishing and beautifying her new piece?

You see, once the tape is removed – that is when it is time to start polishing the piece, perfecting the connections to make it ready for applying the gold, which will highlight the breaks where the piece was damaged. This is the process that will make it obvious that all the labor and time has been worthwhile. This is when the Kintsugi master can embellish and make visible the beauty, uniqueness, and the new strength of the recovered piece.

This process also takes time and care, as the pieces are polished again and again until completely smooth, all in preparation for the powdered gold. The piece begins to take shape, and at this point you can envision the final product.

KINTSUGI IS AN EXHILARATING PROCESS.

Once we have given ourselves the time to create new habits that are improving our lives with the changes we adopt, we start realizing that we feel better and we are growing. We begin to understand why we had to go through the journey we did, and at times we even appreciate the process, including the hardship. Not that we are happy to have suffered, but we suddenly understand why we had to go through it. And as we are admiring the new version of who we are evolving into, we can accept the process that it took to get here.

Think about something that you really want in life. Let's say you want to have a child. You get pregnant and frankly it's not fun to feel nauseous, the back pain, being prodded by needles, the invasion of your privacy at every check-up. Then there is the delivery… and well, it is painful, and your body is not the same… but you look at that precious child that you wanted to have and you are so honored to have been gifted that miracle. Suddenly the pain of the delivery is only the means to your dream. Improving and growing as humans is similar. If you can understand the connection to having a child or achieving any major milestone that requires hard work, you can understand how a person can start feeling that the process was worth it, when she realizes who she has become.

It is a similar feeling when you are building a company. You sleep very little, most will sleep on someone's couch because they are not yet making money, they work around the clock and the uncertainty is tremendous. But then things start to turn around. Customers love your product or services. The company is growing, and your dream is becoming a reality. The entire time of struggle is now only a means to this unreal success that you are experiencing.

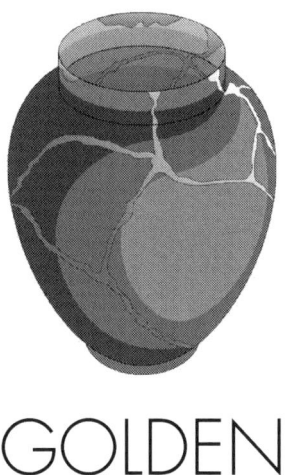

# GOLDEN

It is time for the gold, the beloved and admired metal that is worth so much. Speckles of gold dust are applied to the piece, decorating and highlighting the breaks. It is the moment where the Kintsugi master honors the breaks and highlights all the work done thus far. Weeks and months of meticulous work is not celebrated until finally, the master is able to create the part that all can see. The part that all revere and admire. The part that later she will be able to look back and remember all that it took to get to that point. The gold is the medal that celebrates all of that work and time and devotion, the belief and the strength and the stillness... all now wrapped in gold.

And in real life, it is no different. Those who healed, understood and remembered what it took to get from complete tragedy and brokenness to the point where they can understand the value of the pain, the value of the work; and what they admire now is not only what they have become, but how they celebrate the moments of tears and despair, Ah-has, and the hard work, new habits, the time of stillness, acceptance and listening, the moments of change, and incremental growth... until one day they are able to look back and see the gold, that is YOU - shining now and rejoicing from the entire trajectory.

But the gold is not the ending. The gold is the sudden comprehension that today you are so much more valuable and unique; that going through the pain was a worthwhile journey you had to embark on so you could become the masterpiece you are today. And tomorrow if you break again, you know you are capable of putting your pieces back together. You have what it takes: you are a Kintsugi master. The gold is also the knowledge that you 'can', that you 'are', that you have purpose, that you are special; and that, if needed, you can do it all over again.

## BUT WHAT IS THE GOLD IN LIFE?

The next chapters describe 10 golden nuggets to heal your heart and soul and become the masterpiece that you are intended to be. All the women I interviewed in the past two years have achieved healing by adopting these behaviors, making these decisions and adding these golden nuggets into their lives. These behaviors are a common denominator among Thrivers. They are the guide and direction to ultimately feeling more resilient, strong, unique, and ultimately whole.

ALERT! Reading these chapters will not make you joyful. Reading the chapters is like reading a map, but only if you embrace the road and take one stop sign at a time. If you are fully committed, you are on the road to healing and joy. If you choose to live with intention and work at becoming more joyful, the information will begin the process. You must choose to work hard and implement the steps in your daily life. If you do, you will succeed. Joy is a choice you need to renew each and every day for the rest of your life. Will you make the right choice?

In her best-selling book, *The Secret,* Rhonda Byrne explains the laws of attraction and how we create our destiny by our beliefs, visions, and words. When we live an abundant life, it attracts abundance. If we live a life of joy and fulfillment it will bring more joy and more fulfillment. We attract what we think and feel. We attract our dreams by living as if they have already come true. No one is disputing the law of gravity because there is really no way around it, but the law of attraction requires belief, that is why Rhonda calls it *The Secret*.

You must believe in the law of attraction, and only after believing you can manipulate and implement it to your benefit. Start the process. Believe in your abilities to create the change you want in your life. You can't change the outcomes of your life before first making the change in you. If you do the work, one day you will wake up and say, "I am Kintsugi."

CHAPTER SIX

Golden Nugget #1
# TAKING RESPONSIBILITY

You must take personal responsibility. You cannot change the circumstances, the seasons, or the wind, but you can change yourself. – *Jim Rohn*

If you had the opportunity to learn with Warren Buffet, one-on-one how to invest your money, would you jump at the opportunity? How about if you had a chance to learn music from your favorite and most successful musician/composer? Or imagine how fun it would be to have Picasso or Monet give you a private painting lesson! The idea of learning from those who practiced and succeeded is one that is rather clear. They are considered at the top in their field; of course, I want to learn and model their instruction!

But when it comes to personal changes, we have a habit of saying, "Well, my situation is different, and no one understands my circumstances. My background is not the same; you don't get my culture..."

I said similar things... and that is why I embarked on this self-created and self-appointed research. I needed answers to this voice inside of me, "My circumstances are different and therefore there is no set path to healing. What worked for them will not work for me."

In the past two years I have interviewed women from different religions: Christian, Jewish, Muslim, and those of no particular affiliation. I interviewed women from different countries; United States, Australia, Israel, South America, Britain, France, Canada, India, and more. I have spoken to women from the full spectrum of ethnicities. And I interviewed women with a variety of careers and educational backgrounds: students, lawyers, writers, artists, dancers, models, designers, teachers, stay-at-home moms, stylists, engineers, etc…

Their ages ranged from 23 to 75 and their traumas included amputation, sexual abuse, physical and mental illness, the loss of a loved one to suicide or addiction, and other adversities.

When tragedy happens or adversity strikes, we don't believe that we have guilt in what transpired. When a person suffers a tragedy, abuse, abandonment, neglect, or an illness, we don't consider their responsibility in the event. We think about the hardship, the consequences, the loss, pain, anxiety, depression, PTSD, and much more. It is obvious that they are victims and not really responsible for the event. However, from my interviews, 100% of the women I spoke to who have gone through tremendous ordeals, at some point or another, asked themselves these questions:

> *What could I have done better?*
> *What am I hanging onto that I could let go?*
> *How can I move forward and become wiser?*

*What would I do if I was placed in the same situation again? What changes can I make so this never happens to me again?*

Women who are Thrivers started the healing process by taking responsibility for their reaction to what happened to them and they are not afraid to say, "I also made mistakes and I forgive myself, and I will do the work to find healing instead of waiting for it to happen to me."

We have become a community of people who deflect responsibility; but frankly, we are all responsible for certain actions, words, thoughts, and decisions. If nothing else, we are responsible for how we react to what happens to us. That is something we can actually control. We may have to work at it, but it can be done. Very rarely do we react in the most perfect way.

Taking responsibility has an implied message that we agree that we made mistakes and that we are less than perfect. Agreeing to this seems to be a weakness. It is 100% the contrary. Taking responsibility is the beginning of an empowered journey. The weakness is putting all the responsibility onto others. That leaves us without the ability to change, grow, and improve. When we say, "I am responsible," it places us in a position where we can grow and become more resilient.

Knowing that we can fix something within ourselves brings us back to a position of control. We can't fix others, we can't fix what already happened to us, we can't change the past, but we can control our future and our reactions to our situations.

When I interviewed Loretta, she described a life filled with lies. Not lies that she told others or that hurt others in any way. Quite frankly, Loretta had suffered many hardships. She experienced four bad marriages. Loretta's bad relationships were not really her fault. One marriage happened when they were too young to understand what they wanted out of life; the next, they fell out of love; another, the husband had a mental breakdown and she hadn't been aware that he had struggled with bipolar disorder since childhood. In reality, Loretta could have continued to blame her bad luck and every man that she had met throughout her life. She could have attributed her life story to unfairness.

But Loretta decided to take responsibility for her choices and behaviors; she stopped everything and started learning more about herself. For two years she introspected. She didn't allow herself to meet other men before she took a deeper look into her life and her choices and changed some bad habits and patterns. Loretta's self-imposed time-off was filled with much introspection, she read and actually learned *The Four Agreements* by Don Miguel Ruiz, among all of her other activities.

It was only then that Loretta realized that she had been lying to herself her entire life. She lied about the memories of her mother's death, her brother's death, and how she was making choices.

When Loretta decided to face them, she started to see the possibilities. She granted herself forgiveness and self-kindness, and she worked on her decision-making skills. She decided to face life with all the bads and the uglies. She learned to love herself for who she was, without embellishments. Only when Loretta became aware of her true self, when she noticed her own patterns, was she able to make changes. She became full-on vulnerable on social media when she started her blog[1] and told every story that was a lie so that everybody and anybody could read it. Loretta was not relinquishing her power. She was actually taking it back. She is now happily married, writing her book, and continuing her journey to joy in a very authentic and real way.

Throughout my own journey I have thought about the many actions I took that perhaps today I would have chosen differently. Not that they were wrong or bad, they were just not clear, succinct, or focused on the end goal; you can't force a square peg into a round hole, and at times that is what I was doing. It doesn't matter if you are right, what matters is how it is viewed by others. People have different perspectives and once you understand that, you start seeing things differently yourself, and suddenly something that had the best of intentions and was very obvious to you, was clearly the wrong move to make in order to achieve the best end goal. I too am responsible for my actions.

The most interesting part that I noticed in my own growth was that before I began this journey, I cared more about how the other person grew, changed, and repented. But today, I really don't care about others' journeys as much as I care about mine. Each person has her own storyline and she needs to deal with her behaviors the way she sees fit. It is none of my business if someone is making bad decisions. It is my business how I lead my life, the choices I make, and ultimately the way I show up. We focus on looking at and, frankly, judging others through what is visible via the limited window we have at our disposal. What we should do is add silver to that window, making it a mirror so we can take a deep look at our own behaviors and choices instead of focusing on others.

Once you take a serious look at how you show up, how you interact, what you expect from yourself and others, you will notice things that you should change. Each of us has control over our own shortcomings, and that is a most empowering feeling. We can't change others, but we can always grow and become a better version of ourselves.

Think of it this way: You live with yourself and when you make positive changes to your own character, you'll actually enjoy more the person you have become. That is a fantastic and amazing feeling.

What does it mean to take responsibility? What about a person who was victimized as a child?

Cathy was abused by her stepfather from age six to 12. Is there any responsibility on her part? When Cathy's mother finally discovered what was transpiring under her own roof while she was working the night shift, she confronted her daughter to find out if it was true. You see, Cathy's mom found a letter that her husband made Cathy write as part of her "punishment" during the time he abused her.

Cathy broke down and shared that this had been going on for years. Her mother did not hesitate and immediately kicked her husband out of the house. When Child and Family Services came to the house to discuss what it would mean to press charges, Cathy decided against it.

When Cathy was a child, there was no protection of identity for the minor, and she didn't think that she could survive seeing her name in the media and knowing that everyone would be talking about her and the abuse she had sustained for six years. It was too much for her and so on that day, she decided to not press charges and continue on with her life.

This decision came to haunt Cathy for many years. To think that he most likely continued to abuse others was painful; which made it harder for Cathy to continue her healing journey.

Cathy tried to press charges years later, but it was past the statute of limitations. She kept apprised of where her stepfather was living and at the time that she was ready to confront him, she found out he had passed away.

Cathy had to let go and forgive herself for a decision made when she was very fragile and just 12 years old. But she also understood her responsibility and how her voice could still make an impact. She had a story to tell and one that could still help many. So, years later as a grown woman, she wrote a book[2]. Cathy told her story of abuse and her story of healing. She became a voice for the little girls whose innocence is robbed by monsters in the night.

Responsibility doesn't mean that the "victim" did something wrong. In retrospect the women I interviewed believed that they could have responded better, said something, warned others, reached out, stopped the drugs, visited the parents, found a way to patch the relationships, broken the cycle of abuse, left their abuser, and all those other things that in hindsight are crystal clear.

It is not a reason for blame, no one is pointing fingers, but the change that can be implemented from taking the responsibility is freeing and empowering. Ultimately, we grow. We become stronger, wiser, and more special. We become Kintsugi.

When women take responsibility, it is the beginning step of healing; it is empowering them for the work ahead. It spearheads their tremendous change and growth.

TAKING RESPONSIBILITY IS GOLD.

CHAPTER SEVEN

## Golden Nugget #2
# BELIEF IN A HIGHER POWER

Once you realize there is a Higher Power, you know you're not alone, that you have a purpose on the planet. You control your destiny instead of letting the day lead you where it may. You seize it, take it and lead it.
— Queen Latifah

This is not a book about religion; nor is it advocating that you practice organized religion. As I shared before, I have interviewed Christians, Muslims, Jews, and women who are not part of any organized religion, but 100% of those I interviewed believe that there is a higher power. They believe that there is a reason for being in this world, and that life on this planet is not all that there is.

All the Thrivers I have met with and spoken to, see that the hardships they endured had a bigger purpose and mission. Through their reflection and introspection, they gained a deeper understanding of their mission in this world. Thrivers believe that the reason they are bestowed with the privilege of being here is to accomplish something of value. We are gifted with a life in this amazing world and are able to enjoy so many blessings; but ultimately, the reason for us being here is much bigger than just fun and games.

Once the women understood that the hardship was ultimately bringing them closer to their purpose, they became active participants in their healing. Thriving women like to feel accomplished. They see the value in reaching their full potential as fast as they can.

GREAT CONCEPT. HARD PRACTICE.

Two people can experience the same thing and one can see God/a higher power and the other cannot. I have heard stories of Holocaust survivors who became more pious, bigger believers, and saw the blessings and miracles that came from the horror and the duty to keep the tradition and remain faithful. Others do not see God, and do not understand how He would allow such tragedy to happen and because of that they abandoned their faith, at least in part.

Many people become angry with God when their lives fall apart. They immediately feel forsaken, forgotten, and they question if God is even around us. Maybe He created the world, but He took a hiatus and really doesn't care what we do with it.

My friend, Aliza, has an unshakable belief in God. She is a woman who I admire, and I feel so incredibly lucky to call her my friend. When I called Aliza for our interview, she asked me which of the tragedies that she had gone through would I want her to focus on. Can you read that one more time? Which of the tragedies? Yes, Aliza has lived through a lot, and her love for God and feeling His love for her is the most beautiful and inspiring of feelings.

Aliza was born into a Protestant family, but by the time she was 16 she felt that this particular religion was not her path and went on to discover and learn about the Jewish religion. She started her conversion process and enrolled in the Israeli army soon after. She became a public speaker, a mentor and someone who guides women with questions about faith and spirituality in between many other jobs.

Aliza and her husband had six children, all very different from each other. Her youngest son, Doni, showed signs of mental illness at a very young age. At five he asked why he had to be born, and that he didn't want to brush his teeth because they would decompose underground anyway. At nine years old he wanted to walk into the ocean and keep walking and never come out. Aliza and her husband had their hands full; they had to keep him alive. They took him to all kinds of therapists and tried all kinds of medication. Doni was extremely smart; but nothing could make him feel like he wanted to take part in this world. He never felt like he belonged.

I asked Aliza to talk to me about Doni's suicide. Because this is a taboo subject, people don't usually share the stories of their child's suicide; many even hide it in shame. Not Aliza. She was determined to share her son's story and enlighten us. She was the one who found her son dead. She was committed to be of service and help other families who could be struggling with similar situations and remove the shame and provide unconditional love and understanding for those raising children with mental illness.

Aliza said: "Miriam, people are curious about the suicide. But, frankly, talking about what it is like raising a child with devastating mental illness is really the story. There were times he would be so violent that my husband and I were afraid of him, when we had to call the police to come help us. Those are parts of our day-to-day that no one knew we were living, and the pain and the loneliness were very hard. In death he found peace and obviously, it gives us solace to know that he is no longer suffering. His doctors used to tell us that his mental illness would eventually kill him. That he would probably kill himself (he had tried multiple times before) and that it was not any different than someone who has a heart condition and the heart just gives in."

From my conversation with Aliza, what I noticed most was her unshakable belief that despite the excruciating pain of seeing her child suffer for so many years, she never questioned God. She knew that she could not see the full picture, and that there was a good reason for this event to be part of her journey. Grief has nothing to do with the belief in God, that He is the ultimate of goodness, in fairness, in accuracy, and in perfection. Aliza misses Doni every hour of every day, and she honors him by sharing her story and allowing for the conversation on the topic to be had without judgment.

Interestingly, some of the women interviewed described not having a connection to a higher power until they faced adversity and they healed and overcame their hardship. They didn't feel forsaken through the process; rather, they felt the love and the connection guiding them through it. They describe how they saw God's hand or some higher power of goodness that assisted them in their journey and enabled them to overcome their situation.

The day that my husband and I went to the beach and collected all those shells, when we transferred each pain we were feeling onto them, and then released them into the ocean these words echoed within our healing process:

"What if we are praying for the wrong things?"

What if we are praying for a solution, for clarity, for an end to our pain, but in reality, maybe we just need to go through the pain to get to the other side? When pain is great, we want to move ourselves out of it. It is almost like a boulder in the way and we think that maybe now we want to go around those boulders and take a detour, but we can't.

We have to go through it to get to the other side - to climb each boulder and descend each boulder and sit on them and keep trailing them. My husband and I felt broken. If I tell you it was hard to walk from the car to the sand, I am not exaggerating one bit. And when he looked at me with his sad tired eyes and asked, "So, what should we do now?" I looked at him and said we needed to pray for help to make this process easier, to hold our hands, and to be there to support us. It was obvious we had to experience the pain, so at least we should be supported to be better equipped for success. I do not exaggerate when I say that we saw and felt a huge shift right then and there at that beach.

We started walking with purpose; we felt a lightness in our heart. We felt that we were not alone, and that we had someone walking alongside us, softly blowing the wind behind us, moving us along, and from that day forward we felt that we had a huge support.

Believing in something bigger and believing in the process is something that will accompany you through the healing journey in a very meaningful way.

If you are reading this book and you are working toward becoming a Thriver, but you don't believe in any specific higher being, I would recommend that you read, study, speak to those who do, watch some inspirational videos, and find a way to connect with the higher power. Because the research doesn't lie, every one of the Thrivers interviewed believed in something bigger than themselves. In doing so, this removes them from the center, and from the place of victimhood. It gives them a higher purpose and all of that helps them to find Joy, which is what we are after.

I have seen many miracles in my life. I have witnessed prayers being answered. I have experienced situations in which I had no money and I prayed really hard and suddenly the next week I got a check from a client who owed me money for so many years that I had forgotten about the debt.

Other times we pray so hard for something specific that we feel should be so easy to attain and the answer comes back as simply; NO. Then years later we understand that it was for the best. We simply don't see the full picture while going through the adversity.

I believe that the biggest misconception is that if we pray, we will get what we ask for. That is not the case. Sometimes what is best for us is not what we are asking for. No, you can't get the Porsche or no, you can't get the health you want. It is not because we are less deserving or, because we didn't pray hard enough, it is because we don't see the big picture.

The Titanic is such a great example to describe the concept of the big picture. The Titanic was a huge, luxurious, boat. It was supposed to be unsinkable. But arrogance and a lack of seeing the full picture (the iceberg) caused it to sink.

The boat sped far faster than it should. Fifteen hundred people perished because of what they couldn't see.

We can only see what is out in the open, what our eyes can see, and our ears can hear. The tip of the iceberg is a very small part of its entirety, the biggest part of the iceberg is hidden under water. We may pray for specific outcomes, not knowing exactly what we want, and believe we should have things that are actually not good for us, based on our limited comprehension of how the world runs.

So, when the answer is no, we must remember that we say "No" to a loved one, as well. As a responsible parent, you say "no" to your child who wants to eat sugary snacks all day long. You do not allow that to happen. Your child thinks that you are mean, that you don't understand them and how much they love cake and hate broccoli.

Your view is broader than theirs. You know that if they ate sugar all day, they would be sick, hyper, less focused, and overall unhealthy. Sometimes the answer to our prayers is "No" and the good reason behind it is something that we simply don't see or understand.

That is what faith means; it is a total belief and complete trust that you place in something or someone, and you follow blindly, knowing that the higher power has it figured out and ultimately wants what's best for all of us. So regardless of how we feel about the outcome, we understand that there is a bigger picture that we are not privy to.

**FAITH IN A HIGHER POWER IS GOLD.**

CHAPTER EIGHT

## Golden Nugget #3
# THE POWER OF PATIENCE

Patience and perseverance have a magical effect before which difficulties disappear and obstacles vanish.
— *John Quincy Adams*

I do everything fast; waiting or being patient is not one of my strengths. When I watch videos or take online courses, I speed up the audio because I am just too impatient for the slow process of speaking. I need to consume fast, do fast, get solutions fast. When I type on my computer, sometimes I am so fast that the keys just can't keep up.

At times I think that I am afraid to die before I accomplish all that I want to do. Maybe my brain just works at a fast forward speed and I can't handle the slower pace. I understand fast and therefore I want to move fast.

When I go through challenges, I try to find what the lesson is of each specific test. Interestingly enough, I find that most of my challenges are teaching (or trying to teach) me patience.

In the early days after I found out about Kintsugi, I started looking for a Japanese Kintsugi master living close to me so I could learn from him how to mend a broken piece of pottery. I felt that learning the process would be meaningful and an important part of my transformation.

I found one in New York City his name Gen Saratani[1]; he is actually the only Japanese native Kintsugi master in the US. I found out that he gives classes in Kintsugi and I could not wait to join. When I contacted him, he explained that the classes are a few hours long, once a week for a month.

I wanted to attend, but since I live in Florida it would be cost prohibitive to travel there each week and I couldn't leave my family that often. Instead, I asked him if I could come and spend a full week with him learning the process. His answer was transformational.

He told me that the wait is a crucial time in Kintsugi. It is not just that it needs to dry, but the artist needs to embrace the time. Kintsugi is not just an art form; it is a philosophy for life. Those who live and breathe it understand that the wait is a spiritual journey and a teaching for life.

His response was offering me one of the hardest lessons I had to learn. The lesson of patience, of appreciating the wait. Understanding the wait has a job, a purpose, a meaning, and a value. The wait is the exact time to reflect, grow, and introspect. It is the time where we dig deep, analyze our life's contributions, seeing what we can do better, practice being better. Going over again and again what purpose we have in this life. Visualizing a future of wholeness, and then working toward it. Before you can implement any change, you must sit and wait.

About a year later, I had the opportunity to sit down with Gen and have a face-to-face conversation where I thanked him for the lesson he gave me about the philosophy of Kintsugi. I enjoyed seeing his beautiful work, talking about the Japanese methodology, and learning the lessons that were passed from generation to generation.

Waiting is just that: waiting. It is simple. In fact, so simple that it is not a time for harsh decisions, monumental changes, and drastic choices. It is not a time to move, change jobs, or leave a relationship. This is a time to introspect. That means to sit quietly within yourself and grow from inside. I will admit that it is hard at first, but once you arrive, you will live by your own introspection.

I am somewhat of an artist. I mean, my pieces are not on display in fancy museums, but every wall of my home is decorated with something I have made. Having gone through art school and been lucky enough to have had some amazing teachers in my life, I learned so much about light and dark, color, composition, shapes, emotion, brush strokes, tools, and more.

When you learn about positive and negative space you learn that nothingness, blank spaces on a page, are just as important as the places you fill with art, words or graphics. How much nothing space, (blank space) there is will emphasize and give more importance to the spaces that are filled. And when it's complete, you ask, "How will a person view it, and how much time will they spend looking at it?" Make it too busy, the person becomes overwhelmed and wants to move on; make it too empty, it seems unfinished and boring.

Our lives also need some negative space, and by that, I mean silence, inactivity, and re-connectivity with our inner self. We need silence so we can hear. We need to stop all movement to feel the wind, the sun, and touch the stillness. First, we need nothing in order to feel something. Think about this. We are in a world where people are online 24/7, communicating via social media, making new connections that are mostly superficial, but we don't seem to have the time to disconnect so that we can reconnect. That is, reconnect with ourselves and with our values; and also with the people who are the closest to us and most important in our lives.

We talk about kindness, sharing, and giving. We share our views about understanding and being tolerant. We talk about self-care and mindfulness, but rarely do we talk about being patient. Stopping. Not doing, but being. Not talking, but listening; not thinking, but absorbing; not running, but sitting still; not making decisions, but letting things happen so we can observe and learn. And when our hearts are less impulsive and more coherent, we will make better, wiser decisions with fruitful consequences. Make room in your day for it.

I ask you to give importance to the no action, the negative space, and the wait-and-see-what-happens in that space of nothingness. You will find strength, wisdom, and the voice of your gut feelings speaking to you in a tone and style that has been muted by so much noise that you don't even recognize it as your inner voice, your sixth sense. You can only connect when it is quiet in your head.

Kintsugi is teaching that everything is mendable. It is teaching that the beauty and the value in us is exactly in the scars, as they are proof of a life well-lived and lessons learned. It is what makes the piece and the person unique. It is teaching that if you add gold, you add value to your life; you create a richer life experience.

The time that it takes to build this beautiful piece, or your beautiful life is slow and tedious, but every minute of it is necessary, as it takes patience and a belief in the process to carry out what we are here to achieve. The wait time is a special time that cannot be rushed or skipped. There's no fast-forward button.

Could it be that the lack of patience has a little bit of a feeling of superiority? "Oh, I don't need that much time, or I don't need to learn this or that…"

Could it be that the lack of patience is testing my faith, the belief that there is a higher power who is ultimately in control of things and running the show and that He requires things to go one step at a time? Therefore, is my frustration a sign of a weak faith?

Could the lack of patience in a relationship be a game changer? Are we going to stay connected, in touch, and in love if a lack of patience is played out in our relationship?

How does impatience play out at work, when we skip processes and believe we know enough, have grown enough, and experienced enough? How will impatience affect our health if we don't take time to cook a delicious, nutritious and balanced meal and instead grab a piece of bread and spread some butter on it?

It is not easy to dig deep to answer these questions, and even more uncomfortable to accept the possibility that so much of the adversities we go through are based on the sheer fact that we are impatient to rush through the process. We must learn to be more accepting that things take time. Rome wasn't built in a day and neither will your problems be solved in a quick and clean way. It is just the beginning on the right path to healing.

With time, meditation has become something more common and practiced among people of all walks of life. As we are more influenced by eastern culture and Buddhist rituals, we are starting to learn and speak about the importance of stillness. For people like me with "sparkling" overactive brains constantly creating, thinking, and moving at a faster speed, stopping is immensely difficult. How realistic is it to stop to feel each breath and live in the moment with complete connection and stillness?

As I write this today, I confess that the thought of meditating can be stress inducing. Maybe one day I will grow to learn and appreciate it, but here is a newsflash; there are so many ways to learn to be patient and not all of them include counting breaths. I think about the glowing warm light and try to see and feel it in my brain and within seconds I am also thinking about the laundry that needs to be folded, the client that needs attention, and the dog, was she fed and let out? But patience is not just about being able to stop and mediate or live in the moment; there is a lot that goes into it.

Then comes practice; becoming an intentionally patient person requires effort. Like anything that we want to become better at, we must practice and be consistent, never quitting or getting discouraged, even when we take a few steps back.

Recently, my daughter took up piano. She is 20 years old and when I was paying for a piano teacher at a young age, she did not want to practice, as she didn't have the discipline or patience for it. Now, she has taken to the piano and is self-learning. I believe that through age and maturity she understood what it took to be able to play the instrument and the process became less daunting.

She understands better the reward, and now she is happy to put in the time, the effort, and patience... a lot of it. Singing and playing the same song again and again and again because for the first 100 times it will be choppy and imperfect, but when you keep at it, suddenly the notes roll out of the fingers and the song becomes like a bow on a gift, which makes the experience a joyful and worthy event.

I interviewed a beautiful, thriving young woman named Ashley; Ashley was born with one arm, while her twin sister was born with both. Ashley's parents had to have incredible patience while raising their daughters. One was making strides, moving, achieving every milestone by the book, while the other twin had difficulties. Her parents could have skipped the patience step and done things for Ashley, pampered her and helped her along the way.

However, that would have been a selfish act of impatience. As parents, they decided early on that they would do whatever they could to empower Ashley to live a full life, to show her and guide her to do anything she set her mind to. The only difference was that Ashley would take longer to learn how to maneuver life with one arm, and she would have to deal with some frustrations, including seeing that she couldn't do exactly what her sister was accomplishing. As a united front, her parents would ensure Ashley had the tools to learn and have a wonderful, fulfilling life.

Ashley was raised with great patience, which was the biggest gift she could have been given. She was able to learn how to tie her shoes - with one arm, crawl with one arm, swim with one arm, and cook with one arm. She learned to do everything her sister did, and in some areas she learned more.

Ashley became a professional scuba diver with sharks, a professional dancer, a professional model, and a professional horseback rider. Sports didn't scare her; life didn't scare her because she had received the gift of patience. She had to deal with much pain and heartbreak from those who judged her abilities by her differences, but she was able to show everyone what tenacity meant and what could be accomplished when you are given the time to thrive.

When I interviewed Ashley, she was 27 years old. The mom of a toddler, she described to me how once when she was in a public bathroom changing her daughters' diaper a woman came in and offered to help. Ashley declined her offer. She changed about 20 diapers daily by herself since her baby was born because she was raised with a can-do attitude, so she had figured it out. But the lady in the bathroom didn't have the patience to wait and see how Ashley was navigating that process, nor did she have the belief that this one-armed lady could do something that, to her, seemed impossible.

Ashley was raised to be patient with herself, to know she would have to keep practicing longer at new tasks so she could get better. She learned to never say never. She always believed she was capable. Ashley knew that with her patience, she could figure out a way to work around her differences.

We all have differences, whether it is in abilities, beliefs, or circumstances; we are all differently abled. Patience with ourselves and others can make the difference between success and failure.

When we improve due to our persistence, patience, and tenacity, we see our growth. We see the improvement in the knowledge we now own, how those lessons became part of the fabric of our being. People say that time heals. The time doesn't really heal the wounds and the pain of the tragedy a person lives through.

It is the patience gained through time and experience. The knowledge gained through the process of being patient and allowing for things to take the natural course that actually heals the wounds. The quiet, the wait is an imperative part of healing and it is as necessary as therapy, as faith, as having a support group.

The quality of the quiet time also matters. If a person spends her days crying, sad, depressed, and in victim mode, the time will not help her graduate from victim to Thriver. That is why I say that time alone is not healing; it is what we do with the time.

It is self-reflection, it is the time you implement self-kindness and self-forgiveness. It is the time you take responsibility and kindly open your eyes for other options, other ways; it is the time you accept that there is a bigger picture that you don't understand. The quiet time and the "nothingness" also must be experienced with intention.

When a Kintsugi dish is being mended, it is a time where you have to put your trust in knowing that you did the best that you could and that when dry, the pieces will be strongly attached and you will be able to proceed with adding the gold.

In baking, the dough needs time to rise; in cooking, the meat needs to be marinated. So much in our lives we are waiting, but we must stop looking at the wait time as wasting time. We must learn and understand what is required of us during this wait time, because wait time doesn't mean inactivity or lack of growth, quite the contrary.

It is the time to appreciate the blessings bestowed upon us, time to notice and pay attention to what we have, what we want to achieve and where we are going. It is the time to look at our moral compass and see if it is directed north. It is the time for us to evaluate how we handle our relationships and decide if we are proud of our words, our actions and our intentions.

The way you do one thing is the way you do all things. Time and patience include doing everything with intention. Eating with intention means more chewing, less talking, and appreciating the now. The gift in patience is learning how to be present the proper way. This is the richest and most undervalued time in our fast-paced society.

The amount of patience I have learned is beyond measure. I had none. Today I have some and something tells me that I will keep learning to have more for the rest of my life. It is learning the intangible when my brain is overactive and my feelings of not fulfilling my passions while on Earth, are always at the edge of my skin.

Each of us is tested differently, as we are improving in different areas of our lives. I think I have clarity in my weakness, which is a great beginning. I am surely better. I am proud of that. I am still digging deep. Learning and growing to be still and appreciate the stillness. Taking one moment at a time.

Life's punches can lead us to making rash decisions and quick changes. That is usually because the current situation is uncomfortable, and we want out. We want to move, change jobs, leave spouses; frankly sometimes we want to run away from every part of life.

I have experienced thoughts of getting on a plane, not even caring about the destination, just so I can go somewhere else and let the days move as they please without having plans, without having a responsibility in the world, without having people depending on me. Sometimes I have felt so desperate for someone to take over all decision making. I felt completely exhausted and could not make one more decision in my life. I wanted and needed a change.

That feeling is quite normal. If you are at the dentist and he is coming near your mouth with a huge needle which you know will certainly hurt, you want out of that chair. I think that our fight or flight reaction goes into full force, telling our physical self that we must get out of that situation or we will be in deep waters. Many start experiencing anxiety or panic attacks; our body is screaming – "Get out! Get out! Danger zone!"

So, much like the example with the large needle coming at you, you start thinking of a plan of action, a place to go, a new job, a new career, a new focus. But during that very specific time, our brain is not functioning in a reasonable manner because we are dealing with all of the hormones and messages from our fight or flight instinct.

Without being at our best capacity to make decisions that will prove to be reasonable, it could lead us to bad choices that will have great consequences. We can quit a job that was actually paying the bills and not all that bad, we can leave a relationship that could have a path to healing and harmony, we could start taking on vices that are detrimental to our physical and mental health, we can abandon obligations that carry so many bad outcomes. Some of these decisions and changes can be reversed, but many cannot. Impulsive decisions can affect your life in the worst way and contribute to your situation spiraling out of control.

After Ali[2] had her first baby, she went into deep postpartum depression. So much of Ali's emotional roller coaster came from the disappointments of unmet expectations. She had a very particular image of delivering her baby at home, in the water, and with a Doula not a doctor. That was not to be.

She felt that she lost herself and didn't know if she wanted to keep living her fast-paced celebrity lifestyle. She was not only a celebrity stylist, but she was also a celebrity herself, appearing in "Stripped" (Bravo TV).

The celebrity lifestyle came with constant recognition, frequent events, and a glamorous life, all things that Ali valued and enjoyed. More than that, she defined herself by the lifestyle she led. However, while she was suffering from post-partum depression, she wanted out of that lifestyle and considered changing professions to become a lactation consultant since one had helped her achieve her dream of nursing her baby.

Fortunately, Ali didn't jump into reckless action, but accepted the stillness. She learned to meditate, gave her body time to heal, talked to people who understood, and as she was healing, she discovered something amazing. Ali had a story and a purpose, and she could use her celebrity status to do good things and improve lives.

The idea of becoming a lactation consultant was to help other moms who wanted to nurse but were struggling, and she was able to do just that, and keep the other part of herself: the parties and events, and the social interaction in big ways. Her Instagram changed to one that appealed to moms of young children. Her voice became stronger; not only her physical voice, but also the person who stands up very publicly to demystify the lies that are told on social media: that every young mom has it all together, that the bodies return to their normal tiny and toned self, minutes after labor... all lies. Ali used her voice to tell the truth. She was authentic, and along the way she helped so many other young mothers who felt as alone and disappointed as she had once been.

Sometimes the inactivity, the no-rushing, calm and stillness is what is required of us so that we can analyze, assess and reinvent ourselves to be people with more meaning and more depth in living our purpose.

**PATIENCE IS GOLD.**

CHAPTER NINE

Golden Nugget # 4
# LIVING WITH INTENTION

An unintentional life accepts everything and does nothing. An intentional life embraces only the things that will add to the mission of significance. – John C. Maxwell

We are plagued by behaviors that we repeat and do on a regular basis - these repetitive behaviors are our habits. Some habits are good, and some are very damaging. Replacing a bad habit with a good one is a science in and of itself. In his book *The Power of Habit*, Charles Duhigg explains the process very well. He writes about how to manipulate habits, change them, and work through them to become a person who is living intentionally.

Reading books about changing your habits won't do you any good unless you are willing to implement what you learn. That is why I created my course, Heal with Gold[1]. The idea was to create a space where women could have a safe place to work on their inner thoughts, feelings and behaviors to overcome pain and create a joyful life by moving from a state of victimhood to becoming a thriver. So much of the transformation toward joy is impacted by how successful we are at changing our bad habits to good ones.

To be successful at breaking a bad habit you must do two things. First, you need to replace the bad action with a good action that gives the same ultimate pleasure, gain, or reward. And second, consistently practicing the new habit so that it becomes ingrained.

Imagine a woman who is always five minutes late. In social situations, her friends and family may be annoyed but they get that it is just her way and they work around it. However, at her new job, that five minutes can mean unemployment for her if she doesn't get a handle on it. The reward for being just a little bit late is the recognition she gets, not always positive, but it is distinctive.

To break this habit, she decides she will be ten minutes early to every appointment. She makes the change and still gets the recognition that she craves because she is suddenly considered reliable.

Maybe you will create a new good habit, but you will not eliminate that bad one. To understand what the results or reward you get from your actions are, you must deeply introspect to learn about yourself in a very raw way. A way you may have never thought of before: To be honest and not ashamed to ask yourself the hard questions. To open your mind and assess why you engage in self-defeating habits. Take the time to think about your bad habits; the ones you would like to change.

If someone takes drugs, she may understand that she does so to mask the pain she feels, because of abuse, neglect, or other trauma. If someone eats too much and gains a lot of weight, the benefit may be that she hides herself emotionally and has excuses to not leave her house because she is afraid of showing her deeper scars. When a couple breaks up just when she thinks it is becoming meaningful, usually it is because she is afraid to be abandoned, and so she leaves first.

The point is, some behaviors have deeper meanings than what is obvious on the surface and the "rewards" are not gifts - they are outcomes you unconsciously desire. The behaviors ultimately provide you something that you want to achieve or experience, due to many reasons including, your own fears, trauma, and past history. The "rewards" are "good" in your mind, but they are not really good for you.

When we take time to overview and understand the reasoning behind bad habits, we understand so much about ourselves. Dealing with these bad habits, and replacing them with good ones, will free you from fears, pains, and anxieties and allow you to live a much more meaningful and joyful life.

This is where the second action comes in. Ms. Five Minutes Late will have to consistently practice being 10 minutes early for everything until it is a fully ingrained new positive habit. Some people say that 14 days, or 21 days, or 35 days are all you need for a habit to change. But what if you need just a little bit more time?

I believe that it takes at least 40 days or more, of doing the new action consecutively, in order to form a habit that will make the new behavior become second nature. I have tried eating right for three weeks and in the fourth week, I had a cheat day which turned into a cheat week, then a month and before long, I was back into old patterns.

I have added exercise during three-week challenges, then skipped the Monday of the fourth week, never to return to the plan I was doing. But I also have worked on habits that I stayed focused on longer, and now they are part of my life to the point that I truly miss it (and it is actually painful) if I skip one day. I will give you an example.

In Hal Elrod's book, *Miracle Morning*, he explains how he changed his life by changing his morning schedule and creating a very defined routine. I really wanted to implement that into my life, but I had one very big issue. I am a night owl and waking up at four or five in the morning was out of the question. So, I just didn't do it.

Sometimes, we don't do anything because we can't see ourselves doing exactly what we learned or read someone else did. But I believe that there isn't one way and we are allowed to do what suits us, based on our own personal experiences. I decided that despite not being able to wake up at four or five a.m. to do the "miracle morning," I was going to create a special routine that would speak to me, and that included the specific time that would suit my schedule. I set the alarm clock earlier than usual; but my focus was also waking up about an hour before the rest of my family, giving me quiet time to implement some much needed "me time."

My new morning routine took shape and I did it every day for over 40 days very consciously. I wrote down what I was doing, and suddenly there came a point that I could not skip it. If I had to skip it for some reason, I felt very much like I had missed my morning cup of joe. I noticed that when my husband had a test in the hospital, and we had to leave the house at six a.m., I was up at five, got ready, packed for the day, but had no time for my morning routine. The entire day I felt like something was missing, and I was just a little off.

It had become a habit and when we got home from the hospital and my husband went to rest, I proceeded with my morning routine. When you don't do a behavior that has become so ingrained in your routine, and you miss it, you know the new practice is now a new habit.

I want to emphasize that during the nothingness time you are introspecting and working on yourself. You are not expecting others to change; you are not making drastic changes that are exterior changes, but you are seeing what you can do to get yourself stronger, wiser, calmer, and more resilient. You are working on replacing bad habits with good ones. You are staying put and doing them over and over again patiently without fail. You are embracing the time that it takes to heal in order to become a better version of yourself: to be calmer, make better decisions, and not rush into anything without being in the best frame of mind.

## MY MORNING ROUTINE

When I was dissolving into my darkest hours, you couldn't tell me to get up early, to be grateful, and to be positive; I was not ready for any of that. It was also not a goal, and I didn't even know about the concept of having a morning ritual. I would wake up and run to my desk to immerse myself in work because, as I said earlier, I was using work as my drug of choice and if you told me to go outside and watch the leaves blow in the wind, I would give you a crooked smile and think that you must be out of your mind.

On my good days, calming my brain is hard. Even in my "Joie the Vivre" days, my brain didn't quiet down; in fact, the more I tried to sit still, the more I noticed that my brain "sparkled."

When I felt stronger and I was immersed in my search for healing, I learned about the concept of a morning routine. We get messages when we are ready to hear them and put them into practice. At the time, I was able to start implementing changes that I knew would help me and bring me to the next level of strength and peace.

When I was ready to implement some kind of a morning ritual, I consciously chose what I would like to incorporate. I believe that each person needs to select the things that will work for them. It is not a one-size-fits-all.

To feed my spirituality and connection with God, the first thing I do is say two prayers. I chose them for specific reasons, and I enjoy saying them. If you are not religious, do not follow some kind of scripture, the psalms are not for you, and you prefer to have a direct regular conversation with the Creator, I think that is fantastic. Frankly, it may be even better. I feel like I talk to God throughout my day and so in the morning I felt like saying those two prayers. It takes me just a couple of minutes.

To broaden my horizons: I subscribed to Duolingo language app; I chose a language that I had started learning while in my travels for work and felt that once I moved my production from Italy to Portugal, I started forgetting some of the Italian I had learned. Every day during my miracle morning, I do 15 minutes of Italian practice through the application. I love that I am increasing my vocabulary and learning some grammar. I feel very productive.

To grow as a person: I take 10-15 minutes to read a self-help or personal growth book. I had a goal to read eight books in 2020. Let's just say that I lost count of how many I have read this year just because of the implementation of this new behavior. Reading 10-15 minutes a day really adds up and you don't realize how much you can accomplish just by adding this little bit of time each day. But the biggest reward is the wisdom and feeling of growth; have you heard the saying that leaders are readers? The more you read the more your brain expands, but it's not just the wisdom, it is the feeling of accomplishment. Do you see how in 35 minutes or so I can count so many accomplishments? And this is all before the family has awakened.

I also live in gratitude but decided that I would make a point to write down those thankful moments. I have a hard-cover notebook that I write in each day. The first 5 points I write down are the items that I am grateful for. I have a rule as to what I can and cannot write… they cannot be the big things like I woke up, I can walk, and I can breathe.

I instituted this rule was because I wanted to force myself to look through my day and appreciate the things that happen to me that are sometimes taken for granted, not noticed. I wanted to make sure I noticed them because the next morning I would have to write them down. So, the act of being awake and paying attention gives me a conscious and alert mind to find the good in every moment. The gratitude is not only giving me pleasure when I am writing it down in the morning, but also through each day when I am awake watching, feeling, paying attention, and appreciating every single little miracle.

I am a true believer in attracting what I desire (the laws of attraction). So, after I write what I am grateful for, I proceed to write 10 long-term dreams I have. I write them in present tense. I write the same ones every single day, and as I write them I visualize that dream as if it is happening, as if I am experiencing it; just that thought makes me excited about the day and my future because I feel the experience that I am visualizing. The first few weeks that I wrote my long-term dreams down I was not staying consistent and that was because I would not feel so strongly about some of those dreams. It took me a couple of weeks until I really felt connected with the 10 dreams. I allowed myself to replace them until I felt that I carved out what I believed were my top ten.

ONE BIG GOAL

After I write five things I am grateful for that happened the prior day, and the top 10 dreams I have in present tense, I write down one top goal for the year. You see, as consultant George T. Doran wrote in 1981 in his paper titled, *"There's a S.M.A.R.T. Way to Write Management's Goals and Objectives,"* goals have to be S.M.A.R.T. – they have to be Specific, Measurable, Achievable, Realistic, and Time-related.

So imagine how you are about to celebrate the new year and you make a bunch of resolutions and you say, "This year is my year to..." I wrote down: write a book. Yes, this book that you are reading now, was my 2020 resolution; it was not a dream, it was a goal.

As soon as I wrote it down with black ink on white paper, I asked myself: Is it specific? Yes, I know I want to share the healing journey that I discovered that is shared by every woman I interviewed the last two years. Is it measurable? Yes. I will write each day, find an accountability partner, and ensure that I reach a certain goal to propel myself forward. Is it achievable? Yes, I knew I had to write it, but I would look for editors and a publisher to navigate the world of book publishing and succeed in launching this goal. Is it realistic? Yes, within a year a person can write more than one book if she so desires, for sure a novice can complete one book. Can I split the tasks into a very clear timeline? For sure.

AND SO, I WAS ALL IN.

It is not good to write more than one goal, as we are bombarded daily with so many obligations. If you manage to accomplish that one goal early in the year, you can then add another goal. As you can see, the more you practice this the more you stay focused on the actions you need to take to become a mover and a shaker.

The part that did not stick, yet – Physical Health: I was doing five minutes of stretches. I noticed that I deeply disliked it and frankly I am trying to use polite words to describe how I felt. I would wholeheartedly dread the stretching part and the minutes would suddenly stop. I know I need the physical movement and I know it is critical for my health, but staying consistent with, "I am a work in progress," I am not there yet. I wanted to ensure that I would keep up with my morning routine, and I was afraid that disliking a part of the routine would break my momentum. I wanted to create a new habit, so I had to remove the stretching. Isn't it better to have 80% of something great, than nothing at all? I have purchased a stationary bike, maybe I can start spinning... wish me luck.

When you live life with intention, every decision is measured, words are spoken with thought and consideration, and the quality of your days are different; they have deeper meaning and more reward. I have noticed that after implementing so many of these new activities my days are lived with more intention and regard to the fact that our time on Earth is limited and we want the days to count.

I want my connections with people to be of meaning. I became more discerning with the choices in the friendships I made. It is wonderful to know a lot of people, but if you feel that the connections are meaningless and go nowhere, and you are wasting valuable time on Earth with those connections, then what is the point?

When you live with intention and your actions have deeper meaning, you receive satisfaction from simple things because you know that they are necessary for the bigger picture. If today I sat outside and was able to completely focus for five minutes on the beautiful breeze and the way the trees were moving in such a caressing manner, and then see these moments as time well spent, since if it got me closer to my overall goal. Because I intend to live a life where I appreciate each moment and that includes the environment in which I am part of.

THAT BRINGS ME TO THE POWER OF OUR FIVE SENSES.

Living with intention means paying attention to how our five senses are used in everyday life. Funny enough, we focus a lot on our sixth sense. Now, the sixth sense is very important and valuable; and actually, if we listened to our gut more often, we would be happier... but the sixth sense deserves a chapter on its own (maybe in my next book). The five senses are a bit taken for granted. We are happy that we can taste, touch, see, hear, and smell, but how are we using these five senses in a way to bring more joy into our lives?

TASTE: One example I like to bring up, is my inability to chew. Since I was a little girl, I pretty much swallowed my food. Frankly, I believe it is the speed in which I do things. Chewing takes time and I don't have any because I am always rushing... I am working on it.

Chewing with intention, slowly, while we pay attention to what we are eating, makes us enjoy the food more and the process of eating more. Food is love and so giving it the proper time and attention brings more love into life. Although chewing is only one facet of tasting, we can't ignore setting a proper time to eat, and enjoying the food without other distractions like our phones and videos. In doing so, you can focus on the amazing tastes that you never discovered before and can bring you joy every day if you do so with intention.

TOUCH: When we talk about touch, we immediately think about hugs and the touch from a loved one, but touch goes beyond that. For example, when walking barefoot on the sand, there are the sensory feelings that are comforting and grounding. When we apply cream all over our bodies, it is very sensory and makes us feel very good about the self-care because it comes from self-love.

When we think about babies who have those swaddling blankets, they are soft and comfy, and they make babies feel loved and cared for. We are sensory humans and the five senses connect us to our feelings, emotions and to each other, but we forget to feed our senses and ensure that each day we are satisfying the needs of these elements.

SIGHT: It is great that we can see, and therefore we can move around the world with ease, that is such a blessing, but when we choose to watch scary movies or sad, and depressing ones, our emotions align with what we saw and the feelings that stem from it put us in a flow of bad energy. Now, if we focus on seeing beautiful things that create feelings of love and serenity, that will put us in that calming space and create uplifting energy. That is why what we see has such an influence on our mood.

We see little children laughing or cats doing funny things and that alone can change our mood 180 degrees. Thrivers ensure that they are feeding their senses and raising their energy vibes to that of joy. They are immersed in the work of becoming more and more joyful.

HEARING: The music we listen to can make us shed tears, remember lost loves and past hardships, or it can put us in a mood to get up and dance, and some of us do dance like no one is watching! Right at that moment, our moods shift to one of joy and happiness. Our sense of hearing is quite attuned to good news versus bad news. We want to hear stories of resilience, and hope; and when we do, it motivates us to believe that these successes can be ours as well. Joy has a frequency and we need to intentionally put ourselves in the same frequency. Like tuning in a radio.

I remember clearly when I used to sit in front of the TV after work and be focused on the shows like 48 hours and Dateline. One day, I was pregnant and watching one of these shows, and my husband came into the room and asked why I was transfixed on watching stories of unsolved crimes that included sadness and despair. He told me to think about how those stories were affecting me and our unborn baby. That day was the last day I watched those types of shows. I no longer enjoy sad movies or thrillers that scare me. I am looking for lightness of spirit; I want to laugh or dance and enjoy a beautiful story. I feel so much better and today I look back and don't understand how I could have lost so much time with such dreadful visions.

SMELL: When my daughter was in high school, we found out she had a cyst in her nose that had to be removed. The surgery was simple and when we brought her back home, she said, "Wow! There are so many smells! The house has a smell, my room has a smell, and I can smell all the different foods!"

Until that very day we had no idea that she couldn't smell. That was when we started talking more about the sense of smell. Surely, we all know the smells we hate: spoiled, forgotten food in the refrigerator, or wet clothes left in a backpack. Your wet dog... no one loves those smells, but what about flowers in a garden, or the smell of fresh herbs, or the peel of an orange, how fresh is that? There are amazing smells that wake up our joy-o-meter and we need to ensure that we feed this sense. All you have to do is start smelling, with intention, the good smells around you.

We were given these gifts, but we don't use them with intention. We allow for life to take shape and whatever we see, hear, taste, smell and touch, we take for granted; whatever happens, happens. But what if we spend parts of our days ensuring that these senses are fed with love and kindness and we use them to feel the goodness? Oh, how much better we would feel each day!

The women I interviewed suddenly realized, as they

were growing stronger, and that there is such beauty to be enjoyed, despite their hardship. They were looking forward to enjoying these gifts, but had to be intentional about feeling and experiencing, because they were also in pain. By working hard to live intentionally, they honed a power to see things in a deeper and more positive light. They worked on their habits, they created rituals, and they fed their senses. They stopped taking the goods for granted and that kept them strong and moving forward.

When you live with intention, you accomplish more, you live more fully, and you surely become stronger and more resilient.

**LIVING WITH INTENTION IS GOLD.**

CHAPTER TEN

Golden Nugget #5
# WE ARE BETTER TOGETHER

*If I have seen further, it is by standing on the shoulders of giants.* – Isaac Newton

One of the reasons I wanted to interview Thrivers is because I wanted to find out if the women had something in common that made them more resilient and able to bounce back from hardship. What could I learn from their journey, individually and collectively?

One common trait among them is that they did not feel embarrassed to ask for help, whether it was from a friend, pastor/rabbi, therapist – at times even engaging a pet. Asking for help was a way to empower themselves and become equipped with what they needed to reach their ultimate goal of healing and living a joyful life. We are always better together when we listen to different perspectives, receive emotional support and validation, find ways to appease our spirit, and have a sounding board to bounce back ideas and plans before acting.

I personally like to surround myself with two types of

people. Those I need and want to serve and help, as they give my life purpose; and those women who are a few steps ahead of me in their journey, so I can learn from their experience and fill my "jug of knowledge." I wanted to be surrounded and inspired by them, empowered by their words and full of hope and support to keep me motivated while I was embarking on my own healing journey.

AND I DID.

I learned about the tremendous amount of solidarity, empathy, and hope women can offer others. It is part of doing together: building inner strength. When we listen to others' experiences, we learn the tools, tricks and feelings they applied in their day-to-day interactions that helped them cope with the struggle. I was able to connect what they did to my personal healing. This connection with my new friends brought me joy and I knew I would heal.

Not everyone can do it alone; self-motivation to introspect and find ways to change is hard to come by; and frankly, even if you are self-motivated, think how much better it would be to do it when you are part of a tribe. Other women who are in the same boat as you, with similar hardships, challenges, and difficulties will have different stories, but together everyone shares wisdom, experiences, understanding and validation, which gives you the power to grow your thoughts and feelings and gain inner strength. *(Join our FREE Facebook community Heal with Gold to join our non-judgmental and super supportive tribe).*

Choosing your community, your tribe, should be a thoughtful act where you believe you have something to offer and others have knowledge, input, and love to offer you. Your tribe should be honest, kind, positive, and empathetic to each other's needs and never judgmental.

Individual friends give us validation, perspective, and comfort. I was talking to an acquaintance, we were not very close, and I explained to her a little bit about what I was going through at that time and while I talked, she didn't say a word, but tears streamed down her face. Those tears spoke volumes to me. They were hugs, and I felt comfortable within my pain. I felt validated that my pain was real and this woman before me felt my suffering the way I was feeling it. It was an unforgettable moment. I never expected her to show her compassion in the most vulnerable of ways.

I don't cry that often, so when I do, I guess it stays in my mind. I remember having a moment. This time I let it all out. I called a friend who is also Brazilian. I love her dearly; she is like a sister to me. As I was crying on the phone, she told me to come over. She made coffee, toasted some bread with butter (a very Brazilian thing to eat), and I cried and cried, and after I told her everything that was hurting me, she said, "Thank God."

She found something good in my situation; something that I could not see. Once she pointed it out, it was crystal clear. I could not see it in my mess, but she could. This technique doesn't work all the time, and surely not with all people, but what ended up happening is that I started laughing. I can still hear her voice saying with the same Brazilian accent, "Thank God!" And even today, as I repeat those words, in her sweet intonation, it brings a smile to my face!

My friend was able to take what I knew was an awful situation and make it feel less painful. She put things in perspective for me. She helped me see that it was not permanent, that I was going to get through the situation and that I had to focus on all the good that could come from it, even if I couldn't see it just yet. The 'good stuff' was there because there is always something positive in negative situations.

Throughout my life I have faced some tough challenges. They varied in intensity and consequences. But for the most part, I overcame each issue through resiliency. You know how it is - people expect you to be strong, to fix, to sustain pain. Can you relate to a feeling of exhaustion from being strong? Even the strongest ones break down and just need some extra tender loving care.

On September 26, 2019, my husband asked me where we lived. What? What do you mean where do we live? He couldn't remember and was acting weird, kind of foggy. I told him that he seemed strange and he told me he felt strange… "it must have been his lack of sleep."

After some back and forth with doctors, we ended up at the Hospital on Saturday night, where he was immediately taken for a CAT scan and other tests. That is when we were told that he had a stroke. He was found to be diabetic with his sugar level completely out of control. His blood pressure was through the roof. We spent four days in the hospital, where each day he got worse, until I finally had enough and took him home.

Today, he is a very different person than the one I married. When parts of a brain are no longer functioning, the person thinks differently, acts differently, and reacts differently. That brings a host of problems and it not only affects the patient, but the entire family. Grieving the loss of the living is not a pain that you get used to, despite having had experienced this type of grief before, each circumstance is unique, each disappointment is a fresh one that needs to be dealt with. Our tests don't end as we get stronger and more knowledgeable, but what happens is that the strength and the tools we pick up along the way help us to navigate the wavy and uncharted waters we are thrown into.

The misconception that life is supposed to be blissful, calm, and beautiful is just that, a misconception. A life filled with occasions to travel, watch live entertainment, nourish amazing friendships, opportunities to see the wonders of the world, and so much more; but this is really not what life is about. These are just bonuses that we are gifted with along a journey in which the main goal is growth, development, and opportunities to be kind and loving toward others.

If we adjust our expectations to be more in line with our purpose on this Earth, the pain is less strong and the outcome is easier to accept. Once we understand the goal and purpose of people cohabitating in the world in general, we will understand that the bonuses are just that: bonuses.

Going through this process with a group is the key to making it easier and more meaningful. You have heard the stories: no one on their dying bed regretted not working more, not buying more, not wasting more time with TV or video games. They regretted the relationships they didn't fix, the connections they didn't care for, and the time they missed with their loved ones.

If we have this knowledge that this is what people regret the most, then surely, we should fill our lives with relationships that will be the conduits to joy and growth.

I recently made two friends through Facebook. They are both Brazilian and I think that is how we first bonded; we were in a Facebook group of 100,000 members. The fact that we had our country of birth in common made us connect quickly and the three of us get along very well. We meet at least once a month over Zoom and we send each other messages via WhatsApp all week long. We share knowledge, experiences, and support.

On our first call, we were practicing for a speak-off competition. We each had to give a three minute talk about what we do professionally, and we had to follow a specific format. We were rusty at first. Our stories were not connecting, the two listening didn't get the full picture and suddenly we abandoned our scripts and started talking from the heart, getting it all out. Before long, we were crying through our stories, listening and helping each other improve our speaking skills, all the while showing each other compassion, unconditional love, and support.

Because we had this opportunity to share with complete strangers deep and open wounds, past experiences of adversity, past pains and hurts, we quickly became each other's cheerleaders. It didn't matter that we were in different states, from different faiths, with kids of different ages. What we saw were three women who were trying to be the best humans they could. All three are trying to raise a family the best way they know how, and we are all businesswomen who have a responsibility to help support our families.

We are all very different, but we found a way to connect in a very deep sense. We are all very strong and have experienced deep pain and are willing to be vulnerable by reaching out. We have the courage to try harder and ask for help. The three of us feel we are connected in a safe and loving space. The most amazing thing is that because the relationship started in a place where were going to give each other constructive criticism for business purposes, we are open to also accepting criticism in our personal lives. We may not tell each other we are "morons" as my "shark" friend did, but we are not shy to tell each other to try different tactics or to share knowledge that could improve our lives.

Do you have a support system to connect with? They don't need to solve your problems; they need to be there to listen and understand. Have empathy. Share tears and hugs and cheer you on to show they believe in you and that they are there for you. Ultimately, you will battle through and do what it takes to get out on the other side of your rough time. You will be stronger and more unique than before. Like a most beautiful Kintsugi pottery.

Look around for your tribe. If it doesn't happen as easy as three Brazilians meeting on Facebook, don't give up. Various community groups or activities will place you with like-minded people. We have created the Heal with Gold Facebook group and welcome you to join for love, support and much wisdom from all of our public speakers. It's a free Facebook page to get all the support you need.

Sometimes we work better and harder when we pay for it, and when we are held accountable. When you make an announcement, "I am going on a diet," or "I am writing a book," you are sending these messages out to the world. Others hold you accountable, checking to see if you reached your goal like you said you would. This might sound weird, but if you pay to have someone check in on you and your progress, you will find that you will complete certain tasks at a much higher success rate. The point is that at times a free support system is not enough. You may choose to find a therapist, a coach or take a course[1] that will help you in your growth journey.

Having people who you trust and feel comfortable to share, vent, and get feedback will move you forward with your goal. That is why the togetherness is imperative for your successful healing.

All the women interviewed found their tribe. If they didn't have family support, they created a chosen family; they hired a coach, a strategist, a therapist that was focused on resilience. It is not always about dealing with the past and the traumas, it is also about figuring out a way to move forward and get stronger.

When Elisheva understood that she couldn't have kids due to her RH factor. She kept losing her babies and felt very alone. She and her husband then decided to try surrogacy but being religious they were afraid of their community's judgment. Luckily, they moved to a very warm, loving and non-judgmental community, and she was able to celebrate the birth of her twins via surrogacy with so many friends cheering her and being happy for her two bundles of joy. This made a world of difference in her journey.

Elisheva told me in our interview that ultimately everything happens at the right time because being where she was and having the amazing friendships that she had at the time made the entire difference in her trajectory.

April[2] was abused by her husband, who suffered from paranoia, drug abuse, who also had cheated on her, when she finally had the strength and a proper plan to escape, she counted on the friends she had made in the school where she was teaching. She needed help to find living arrangements and she needed some people to know what was going on in case something bad happened. Fortunately, she found her teaching community was full of people who loved, admired, and supported her through that very difficult and turbulent time of her escape.

Is it possible to do it alone? Sure, it is. But it will be harder, lonelier, and certainly take more time. Needing help is not a lack of courage; it is not a weakness; quite the opposite. Asking for help shows strength; it means that you are courageous, determined to succeed, and willing to take the journey.

It means that you did not give up on yourself and that you are doing what it takes to succeed.

DO IT TOGETHER, BECAUSE HAVING A TRIBE IS GOLD.

CHAPTER ELEVEN

## Golden Nugget #6
# VANTAGE POINTS

We can complain because rose bushes have thorns, or rejoice because thorns have roses. – *Alphonse Karr, A Tour Round My Garden*

*A vantage point means a position or place that affords a wide or advantageous perspective; viewpoint: to survey a valley from the vantage point of a high hill.* (Wikipedia).

When we are taking stock of our lives and present situations, we tend to look at it head on. Then we look at it from side to side, and up and down. We feel like we are in the valley and cannot escape everything that is coming at us. When we are at war, we cannot plan the attack and cry victory at the same time.

If you feel like you are drowning, you will not be able to view the bigger picture. That is why in history, civilizations have built their fortresses on mountain tops, because from there they could see the big picture. They were situated with a better vantage point.

It is difficult to see the big picture when you are immersed in it. Changing your perspective is a tool that can be a lifesaver, especially if you can change while you are still going through the hardship. The women in my research all used this tool in order to pull themselves out of the victim mentality and start the work toward becoming more joyful. Certainly, when it comes to healing, looking from the big picture vantage point can be the one thing that gives you the opportunity to consider forgiveness, understanding, letting go, and ultimately – healing.

When I started my Kintsugi clothing collection, I had two goals. First, I wanted my clothes with the Kintsugi art to be a reminder to each woman that she has what it takes to put her pieces together, that she is capable of healing, and that she will become more beautiful and special than ever before.

Second, I wanted women who saw someone wearing one of the Kintsugi pieces to be reminded that we are all fighting our own fights. Each of us has a story and maybe a struggle we are dealing with, and if we keep that in mind, we would find it in our hearts to be kinder, softer and more understanding to everyone. We would be more empathetic toward others who are suffering. How wonderful it would be if we could become each other's cheerleader!

The reality is we have no idea what other people are going through and what it takes for them to triumph. We don't see the daily work, the daily hurt and the daily commitment to change what someone else is going through. The interviews with these women showed me true warriors and heroes. It showed me the extent of what is humanly possible even though I may perceive it as impossible.

Thrivers intentionally change the path they are on so they can view their trajectory from a different perspective. By doing so, they become more tolerant and patient, more accepting and loving of people in general.

Changing one's perspective is a conscious action, it takes effort. It seems easier than it really is, and it can create miracles. Here are a few simple examples of how changing perspective can change your reality:

You are on your way to work, driving and minding your own business, listening to a great podcast or that one song that gets you going, when a car comes out of nowhere and cuts you off. You make a hard stop and a sharp turn of the wheel, as your heart pounds out of your chest. As you look in the rear-view mirror, glad you escaped an accident; your fear quickly turns to anger. You are livid with the person who cut you off. You may even want to speed up and give them the finger, scream through your window, or something more dangerous in retaliation. All of that takes you away from that centered place you were at just minutes before you were cut off. Now you are wasting your time being mad that you almost had an accident because of someone's irresponsibility.

Think about that: you are angry because you almost had an accident. Why not be joyful that you almost had an accident, but didn't, and you and your car are on your way to work? If your perspective is positive and joyful, you will flip your feelings from total panic to feeling blessed to have escaped a potentially deadly accident. This is where you blink your eyes and smile rather than squint and curse.

I interviewed a man from Brisbane, Australia named Martin Howard[1]. He organizes meetings between convicts and victims for the purpose of healing and reducing recidivism, and he told me how much healing comes from these encounters. The victims don't meet their own perpetrators, but they meet others in a safe environment where they can connect and ask questions.

The perpetrators interact with victims and observe the damage that was caused on other people by the lack of respect for human life. And the victims interact with the convicts understanding that most always these people are damaged by their own pasts and have a lack of empathy and the ability to relate in a healthy way. It helps both sides.

Martin told me how after the meeting, the victims don't condone the act that happened to them, but they release the anger and pain that they had been harboring in their hearts. They see from the criminals that they have no feelings toward those they hurt for the most part and that they are indeed people damaged by their painful past.

So many of them were victims themselves and something snapped, and they don't have the ability to make better decisions. That is not an excuse for their behavior, and no one is condoning what they have done, but it does put things in a completely different perspective.

Once the victim understands the type of person the perpetrator is, even if he is still thought of as a monster, the victim somehow internalizes it, knowing the circumstances. Some victims ask themselves if the hatred is a worthwhile feeling to endure since in reality, that awful feeling is only hurting one person; the victim. It is not hurting the perpetrator. Their new perspective helped the victims release their anger and start to find joy again.

You need to take control of your situation to completely heal. At one time I felt completely misunderstood by people who I believed were supposed to stand by me. I felt that when I needed them the most, they were not there for me, as I believed I would have been for them. I felt so alone and, in a way, betrayed.

They thought they knew what was best for me. I know now that their intentions were pure, but their actions hurt me deeply. I figured the best thing for me would be to distance myself from them. If I were lonely it would be my choice and not theirs. When you feel in control of the situation, even if the situation sucks, it is your choice and you have no one to blame and somehow knowing that hurts less.

The way we talk to ourselves and what we focus on are our choices, and that can take us either to despair or a great place. Every cup is both half full and half empty. Focusing on the full half is what will change the perspective from victim to survivor to Thriver. The Thriver begins by changing her perspective. Her focus in not on being right, it is on being happy and willing to practice what it takes to achieve and maintain joy and reach her goals.

Our brain has tremendous power. We usually take this power away. We are spiritual beings living a physical life, having a human experience. We forget that we have the power of our spirit to tap into it at any time and create the reality that we want.

LET ME EXPLAIN.

I have TMJ and when it flairs up, I clench my teeth so strongly that I cause myself to need root canals. They are costly and very painful. Because I have had quite a few root canals, and I know they are not fun, I had to create a way to get over them with minimal emotional damage. Here is what I do while seated in the dentist's chair.

I say "I am strong, and I accept this pain with love, and I have the power to sustain this process. The loss of money will be the worst part and I will not allow the pain to take over". Once in the chair, I start envisioning a beach, calm waters, and a warm and inviting sun hugging my skin. I feel the love from God and His hugs. I then concentrate on the wind that the equipment lets out and I start imagining the breeze on my skin and the comfort I feel and I tell myself it is more love and more hugs and I keep talking to myself as I describe the beach in my mind with such great detail that I really feel it. This allows my mind to focus on something so wonderful, as opposed to something painful.

Cathy shared with me the story of her six years of abuse at the hands of her stepfather. Throughout that time, she chose to focus on the good in her life. She chose to see the cup half full.

The exercise that she did as a young child prepared her for a life of finding ways to see things more positively. The more Cathy did that, the more it came easy. I began to notice the same thing with the other women I was interviewing. Most of them are happy that they had to go through adversity. Not because it was easy or simple to overcome, but because when they overcame their adversity, they became someone so much more amazing than they were before.

Leslie[2] was six years old when she ran from her neighbor's house, where she had been playing, to go home and get some more Barbies for their games. That is when the ice cream truck ran her over. The driver didn't see her. Leslie lost her leg in the accident. When I interviewed her, she said the most amazing thing that left me in complete awe. She said: "Can you imagine how the driver felt? He was an 18-year-old on his first day of his summer job, he must have felt terrible."

If anyone could look from a different perspective and make an effort to see the picture from a much different vantage point, it was Leslie. Even today, she shares with me that she is grateful for that day and what happened to her, as it led her to a life of purpose that otherwise she would not be living.

There are three sides to every story: Yours, Theirs and the Truth, not because anyone is lying or deceiving, but because none of us knows the full picture. None of us can see the bottom part of the iceberg because we just don't have that vantage point. We can't see and understand every angle, every intricacy of people's pasts and background.

With a little faith and a lot of strength, and with the commitment to joy and living a happy, fulfilling life we can understand it and create the necessary scenario to ultimately take us to a place where we can see things from different perspectives. Whether we make them up to make us happy or because we know that they are indeed possibilities. At the end of the day all that matters is working on living a full, joyful life and understanding that we don't have the full picture.

If you could ask a Kintsugi pottery piece if it would prefer to be the same original self over being Kintsugi, what do you think it would say? Let me go back to be whole and complete as I was before? Surely not, because the gold and the scars are exactly what is making the piece more unique, and more valuable than before. The same happens with us. After we transform and heal, we look back and notice that as great as we were before our adversity, when we change, there is no comparison.

It is important to make the point that when a person is in the midst of her test, trial, or tribulation, it may be very hard to envision the other side, to look from different perspectives. Remember that these women were sharing the path to joy, some of them were able to keep themselves seeing the cup half full in the midst of the adversity; but most of them used this technique later, when they were safe and on their way to finding a way to reconcile what had happened to them.

There are many types of problems and obviously many types of people. What was very interesting to me was that perspectives were part of all of them at some point or another. Giving people the benefit of the doubt at times is a gift that you give yourself. It allows you to fill your mind with more positive possibilities. Your thoughts direct your journey. The more positive your thoughts are the more beautiful your journey will be.

What we think about is our choice, which depends on our focus and our perspective. Do we want to see from the walled in valley or do we climb the tallest mountain and see the big picture?

And, if we can't see the big picture, we can surely choose to imagine a positive response to our situation. Our thoughts are our choices. We choose our response to life's challenges. We control how events and people will impact our day. You get to choose joy. You can choose a positive grateful attitude. Choose better. Change your perspective!

VANTAGE POINTS ARE GOLD.

CHAPTER TWELVE

## Golden Nugget #7
# LETTING GO

If you want to fly in the sky, you need to leave the Earth. If you want to move forward, you need to let go of the past that drags you down. – *Amit Ray*

This may shock you, but I believe the word forgiveness is misused and overused, and, at times, it really upsets me. When people say forgiving is the biggest gift you give yourself, could it be that we are potentially bullying a victim to do something they are not able to do?

I think of women who were gang raped, like Madeleine[1]. She was raped by three men at the age of 11. I think of women who were verbally, emotionally, physically and sexually abused by their spouses or suitors like Jacqueline who was abused by her military boyfriend. What about those who lost someone in an accident because of a drunk driver? Should they forgive the assailant? I often think of people who survived a terror attack. I know that I cannot comprehend the degree of their pain and suffering. How could I tell another person who was victimized to forgive?

Because "forgiveness" didn't ring right with me, I decided to delve into the subject and try to wrap my head around why it bothered me. I understand the concept of letting go of all the pain and anger and hurt; and yes, letting that all go is a blessing and a gift and should be worked on, but is that really what forgiveness means?

The question about forgiveness is one that I have asked every woman I interviewed, even those who suffered an illness and could not blame anyone but God. I asked: "Do you forgive?" I received two types of responses. One is a simple "Yes, I forgave, I let go of all that pain and suffering."

The second one that I heard from many of the Thrivers is: "We can't forgive the unforgivable, but I let go of the anger and the pain and the hurt. I don't let my mind be consumed by what that person did to me because otherwise, I would still be attached, connected to that person and my goal was to break the chain."

When we think about God forgiving our sins, it means that He erases what we did and we start over; we turn a new page, and our life is a blank slate. There is absolution, there is pardon. God doesn't forgive unless we ask for forgiveness and repent; then we work really hard to not commit the same sin again. Most times we do commit the same sin and we repent again, and we work very hard to be better next time, as we fully intent on becoming better humans.

If you don't ask for forgiveness, if you don't have an awakening, you are not seeking improvement. There is no absolution for the misguided actions. It is just as it is.

I would like to believe that God is sad for the bad choices I make, but still loves me. We learn from consequences; if I don't follow the law and get caught, I pay the price; I have consequences for my transgression. If I eat too much, my belly aches or I gain weight. If I go out in the sun without protection, I hurt my skin. The concept of cause and effect of behaviors is something that we have understood since childhood.

When we tell others to forgive there is a misunderstanding that the act is condoned, absolved and that there are no consequences. That is a very difficult concept to accept. Only the victim can determine if, how and when to "forgive and forget" their adversity and their adversary.

However, we should lovingly grant forgiveness to ourselves for our mistakes and misjudgments, because we know that we want to be better, do better, and grow. We were not malicious, and there is real regret that we didn't make the right choice. We can only achieve and attain our goals if we forgive and accept ourselves, and ultimately, we are able to move forward in our growth journey.

We understand that in every situation we encounter we have some responsibility for our reactions and responses. Every fork in the road throughout all the bumps we encounter, we have choices, and sometimes we don't make the best decisions. We must forgive ourselves and then we must put in the work to improve and return to the right path.

I shared Cathy's story about regretting not pressing charges against her stepfather who abused her for six long years. She was faced with a decision when she was 12, at a time when children were not given privacy rights and were not treated with great sensitivity, and at that time she couldn't move forward with a trial.

As she grew older and saw things from a different perspective and worked on herself, she realized she should have pressed charges because she believed a person like her stepfather would keep molesting and she would feel responsible.

That guilt can be devastating and paralyzing and in reality, it is unhelpful. Often, we make decisions with the tools we have at the time; when we judge ourselves much later, we must remember that we did the best we could with the tools we had.

Then we empower ourselves to do what we can to overcome the bad decisions from the past and make better choices, as Cathy did. She wrote a book, became a public speaker, and works very hard for the rights of abuse survivors and children's rights.

When Madeleine was 11 years old and went with a friend to a bar, she ended up getting gang raped. She had to forgive herself for going to a place where a child should not have been, for lying to her parents, and for many other little decisions that led to that fateful night. But does she need to pardon the rapists? She may have, that is not the point, the point is when we tell people they should, do we fully comprehend the extent of what we are asking them?

When I experienced the loss of contact within my family, I could have continued blaming myself for the wrong choices I made, or I could change, grow, become wiser and then forgive myself for my reactions. This gift of forgiveness sets the scene for exponential growth. When we allow this absolution to happen, we are also focused on becoming better and we set to work on improving our qualities so we would never be in a similar situation again. We already paid for the consequences of our actions and decisions.

Self-acceptance and self-forgiveness come from maturing and growing wiser and being able to see things from different perspectives. We must forgive and understand so that we can move forward with our growth and development.

But what about forgiving a perpetrator, someone who has done the unthinkable? Someone who has committed a terrible crime? Earlier I mentioned that Jacqueline[2] was abused for two years by her military boyfriend. At the end of their relationship he choked her to the point that she had an out of body experience. He held her captive mentally and physically.

The abuse continued even when she managed to leave. He literally terrorized her. When I asked Jacqueline if she forgave him, she said: "Miriam, we don't forgive the unforgivable, he never repented. But I let go. He is no longer the captain of my ship. I am no longer captive, and I am free to live a fulfilling and joyful life."

I asked women who had experienced all kinds of trauma about forgiveness and the more I asked, the more I realized that there is a huge misconception with the meaning of the word. In reality, the freedom that we get is from letting go and disconnecting the brain and heart from the tragedy or occurrence.

You are not saying that the action was acceptable; you are not saying you condone the behavior itself. All you are doing is disconnecting yourself from the person who caused you so much pain, by breaking the tie of hurt, anger, and hatred. Those feelings are binding us to those who caused us pain and ultimately that connection is only hurting the victim.

We want to elevate ourselves, and it is impossible to do so while we are carrying pounds of luggage disguised as the suffering stored in our hearts. That hatred and sadness is baggage that we are trying to carry while we are running the marathon of our life. It is physically impossible to soar with all that pain and hurt attached to us.

How much lighter are we going to feel when we simply let go and allow for the pain and hurt to drift away from our hearts and souls! That is what people mean when they say that forgiving is a gift we give ourselves. I see it as the gift of freedom; it is the disconnection from the negativity that we harbor that will ultimately allow us to unload the heavy and limiting thoughts that stop us from finding joy.

## THE POWER OF WORDS

Words have emotion attached to them. The word forgiveness and the term letting go can't be used interchangeably. They carry a different weight and it is important to choose what is right for you to move past your adversity.

It is crucial to speak to ourselves in kind and gentle ways using words that positively resonate with our situations since the choice of words can be the difference between a life of joy or one of sadness... Thoughts and words are vibrations, they carry energy, and as mentioned earlier, the laws of attraction are just that: laws. If we speak angry, hurtful things, if we are storing hate and disgust toward ourselves and others, we are attracting more of those feelings and situations into our lives.

Think of the children raised by parents who encourage them regularly and believe in their ability to do great things, while others who are told that they are stupid and constantly discouraged. Each child will become what they believe.

When Leslie lost her leg after the car accident at six years old, she was encouraged by her loving parents to keep going, doing, and being. And so, Leslie went on to become a professional skier and then a lawyer, and today, an advocate for kids around the world who do not have the ability to get prosthetics. She has a children's book out and she is really changing the world, one kid at a time. This is because her parents made a decision to use empowering words and give Leslie every chance that she would need to thrive as an adult.

Melanie's story was probably one of the hardest ones for me to write. Her husband had brutally raped her at gunpoint and then shot himself in the head while over her. She ran out of the house naked, splattered with blood, traumatized, and filled with terror.

That same day Melanie had to sit with her kids and tell them that their father was dead. But she wanted to preserve the memory of their father in their minds and protect them from the trauma of the event.

On what probably was the worst day of her life, she had to let go of the anger and hurt, at least momentarily, in order to present the situation to her children. How could she tell them what happened without causing her children to hate their father? Melanie could not condone or absolve what he had done to her, but in order to protect her kids, and to ensure she had a chance at a happy life, she had to disconnect herself from the anger and hate, as well as the disbelief of the nightmare that he had created.

Otherwise, the anger would take away her life forever and that was something Melanie was not willing to do. She had to go through a process of learning to deal with the trauma of the event, while at the same time finding a soft place in her heart to protect her kids from the reality that had occurred. She chose to embrace the rest of her days and fill them up with love and joy. Letting go of the anger, the hurt and the pain would have to be a big part of the process.

I learned something fascinating in my immersion into the world of self-help and interpersonal growth. I learned that there are many roadblocks that cause a limitation in abundance; not only financial abundance, but abundance of goodness in general. Many years ago, I reached out to a holy person to discuss the incredibly hard financial struggles that my husband and I were experiencing at the time. He asked me if I was harboring anger toward anyone. I didn't think of anyone in particular. He told us to take a hard look at all our relationships and think about uncomfortable situations that caused us pain and anger and assess if we were still upset at the person.

We took the homework very seriously. We sat down with our phones and reviewed the names of each person in our contact lists, trying to find if either of us was harboring pain toward anyone. Very quickly we got to a name that I said, "Okay. This person did something I do not tolerate. I have zero patience or acceptance for the behavior. I really believe he was wrong on so many levels."

Years ago, I hired the brother of a friend to do a job in our backyard. He took our down payment, and then took his time in doing the work. When he finally came, he did a small part of the job and then he disappeared. The work had a deadline, as we needed what he was building for a special occasion on a specific day, which could not be moved.

We contacted his brother who was our friend, and we pleaded with him to help us by talking to his brother he had so highly recommended. What he did next shocked me, as well as hurt my feelings. He spoke badly about me to my husband. I was so upset and angry. When I thought about it, I could not give him the benefit of the doubt or find any perspective where he would deserve some kindness. Why would anyone bad mouth a wife to her husband?

I see marriage as a holy union that must always be respected. To me, a marriage is like a temple that God lives in, as He does in all marriages.

Talking about me like that behind my back was unacceptable. And obviously, I had work to do. I had not forgiven him even though with time I thought I did. I was harboring anger and hurt. I couldn't move forward. It was blocking us from our overall good feelings, our energy was not in a good place and it was surely blocking abundance. We want an abundance of peace; we want an abundance of joy, and we want an abundance in financial freedom. But when we harbor hate and hurt, we cannot achieve that because the frequency of abundance is one of joy and love, not hatred and anger.

It is interesting when you take time to analyze all of these feelings that you thought were in the past come back to the surface and you realize how you really feel. And many of these thoughts are hidden in our subconscious, we are not sitting day in and day out hating that person, but inside is a different story, we have much anger and pain.

When we harbor anger, hatred, and bad feelings in general, we are living in a constrictive state of mind. We block the goodness that could be coming our way. When we let go, we not only free ourselves from bad, heavy feelings, we also open up a passage of abundance in every area of our lives.

Choosing to release constrictive feelings that ultimately only hurt us is that exact freedom that we get when we let go. If calling it forgiveness works for you, then forgiving it is. The point is really the results that we get. After interviewing so many women who look so average and ordinary, I realized that they are not at all average but rather quite extraordinary; I became more sensitive to how we, without intention, expect heroic behaviors from them.

LETTING GO (OR IF YOU PREFER TO CALL IT FORGIVENESS) IS GOLD.

CHAPTER THIRTEEN

## Golden Nugget #8
# ATTITUDE OF GRATITUDE

If you count all your assets, you always show a profit.
– Robert Quillen

Feeling gratitude and not expressing it is like wrapping a present and not giving it. – William Arthur Ward

Being grateful when life is going well is not so hard. It still requires a commitment to gratitude, and saying it out loud still requires intention, especially through some bumps in the road. But what happens when life tests you in the most meaningful parts of your life? When adversity strikes taking away from you what you thought was your superpower? What happens when the things you hold most dear are no longer? Can you still be grateful? How and what does it mean?

Every year, 15 million people suffer strokes[1] worldwide, of those, 795,000[2] are in the United States. 5 million die and another 5 million are permanently disabled. There are some that are affected in their physical abilities, as parts of their bodies become paralyzed. To others it is more cognitive, memory loss, constant fatigue, Aphasia and more.

My husband is part of that statistic. As I am writing this book, we are approaching the one-year anniversary of the day he asked me where we live. The changes have been hard for both of us in very different ways. I am still navigating the loss of the person I married and knew for 30 years, while he is trying to navigate his feelings, emotions, abilities and the reality that he could have died.

I remember being at the hospital, after finding out he had a stroke, learning that he has diabetes and hypertension. Being that he eats super healthy, is thin and never had any symptoms we were shocked to the core. There was one sentence I repeated every few minutes. I said it out loud, with a Brazilian accent, as my friend Ana had done for me years prior. "THANK GOD! Thank God you are alive, Thank God you can walk, and Thank God you recognize me. Thank God, Thank God and Thank God..."

I am sharing a painful part of my personal life to talk about the importance of gratitude. It seems counterintuitive but, I learned from the women I interviewed about having gratitude for the hardship and how to be grateful for exactly the thing that broke your heart. That is true gratitude.

It is believing that what happens is for the best and that despite not knowing why or how, we believe in the process and do the best we can under the current situations. I am dealing with my adversity by implementing what I have learned. There are days I do better than others, but the goal is to stay focused on the ultimate win: A joyful life.

## HOW TO BE GRATEFUL

I have mentioned in my morning routine description that gratitude is part of my daily life. When most people think about gratitude, they start with the obvious. I am grateful I woke up today, I can walk, I can breathe, my heart is beating... but these get old fast. They shouldn't, but how many times can you say that you are grateful for being able to see, hear and feel so incredibly connected to this blessing?

Like it or not, we start saying these things from the mouth and not from the heart. The concentration you need to have when saying what you are grateful for, or when you write it in your journal is deep and meaningful; only when you are really connected and you really mean it, will gratitude flourish within you and turn into a deep sense of joy.

I started forcing myself to look for the smaller blessings within my day. I write down at least five things I am grateful for that happened the day prior. I do not repeat any blessing. Each item has to be unique. So, when, at the end of the year, I review the list, I would find 1,825 bullets of gratitude.

In the beginning it was hard to say that I was grateful for the stroke. But I am grateful for the improvement, I am grateful for the new people I have met on this new path we are journeying together. I am grateful for the extra patience I have learned to have. I am grateful for kind doctors who really care. I am grateful for the people I have been able to impact and help by sharing our experience.

When forcing myself to be emotionally awakened, I found that realizing tiny blessings, and some not-so-tiny, they adorned my days, my life. I have a choice to be immersed in self-pity, to feel betrayed by God, to have feelings of unfairness; or I can be curious to see what is in store and live this new life open to the blessings it will bring.

When I changed my thoughts and behavior, I noticed that I was so blessed. So many wonderful things were happening to me each day. I noticed blessings that had nothing to do with the stroke, like quickly finding a great parking spot in the shade and finding a pen that I can write so beautifully and legibly with.

I notice that when I got a testimonial, be it for my apparel line, my course, or a compliment by a friend, it made my heart sing and I was so grateful for those people who took the time to tell me how much I impacted their lives. The wider I opened my eyes and my heart, the more clearly I saw a life full of blessings. Going through adversity, sometimes the noise doesn't allow us to see how our lives are sprinkled with amazing blessings that are pure signs of love.

I realize that I have experienced a loss, but in many ways, I have experienced a gain. I can choose to see the thorns or the roses, I can choose to see the cup half full or half empty. It is my rose; it is my cup of water. It is my life and the choice of being grateful for what I have is mine as well. There is newness to be grateful for and we just need to be awakened to see and internalize that even in the midst of hardships, we can find sparkles of gold to be grateful for.

A WINNING ATTITUDE IS THE VERY KEY TO A WINNING LIFE.

I write to people of all religions, but I tend to go back to the teachings I have been learning since I was a little girl. In my religion the first thing we do when we wake in the morning is thank God for returning our soul to our body. We are supposed to do that before we put our feet on the ground, surely before we take the phone from our nightstand and check out what others are having for breakfast and what resort they are staying in (and at times being jealous about).

Before I wed, my father told me that most couples are unhappy. My father was an optimist and he had a beautiful marriage with my mother, full of love, devotion, and dedication. The underlying message was that my happiness was in my hands and that of my husband, that a happy marriage is a choice we have to make each day (assuming that no one is abusive or narcissistic).

A happy marriage doesn't come just by being together, but by what we do, how we relate to each other, and how we respect each other. It comes from counting blessings, like we may count pennies. People want to get married and have a partner but often after the honeymoon, the relationship goes out the window.

You mean I need to be nice to this person who leaves his underwear on the floor? Like, really? Can't he put them in the hamper? Why do I need to unload all the dishes from the dishwasher day in and day out? Is he not eating here too?

Imagine if you add to it frustrations that come from illness and changes that we have no control over. It is when we focus on the negative stuff and not on the things we are grateful for, that the unhappiness begins to settle into our hearts; then we wonder if we made the right decision and if we found the right partner.

Be it in marriage or in business, relationships with others and with ourselves are extremely hard. It is all about how you see the tiny blessings. Growth happens through adversity, not when things are smooth sailing and easy. Growth can only happen when we are not feeling sorry for ourselves, but when we embrace our new reality. See the good that comes out of it and be open to learn what is in the new path that lay ahead of you.

When I began to consistently do my morning routine, being grateful and taking stock of my blessings became the first thing I wanted to do. The fact that I focus on little things makes me pay attention throughout my day so I will always have something to write the next morning; but more than anything, it teaches me to find blessings that are embedded in the hardship. Having this skill has been imperative when dealing with issues in business, figuring out how to live through a pandemic, and dealing with interpersonal relationships that are far from what I dreamed they would be.

Amy had a great job, she was a runway model and loved the world of fashion, her shoe collection was something spectacular (while I define myself by jeans overalls, Amy surely defined herself by stilettos). She also met the man of her dreams during one of these shows. They wed, started a family and moved from England to Canada. One winter night she was nursing her newborn while the family slept and that is when she realized that her house was on fire. She saved her family and while standing outside, they saw their entire life burn to the ground, including Amy's shoe collection. That may seem like a little detail, but one that plays a big part in her future.

Amy, her husband, and their children moved to South Florida after the fire to rebuild their lives in the sun. With a new job and many dreams, they began the new phase of their lives. After a camping trip, Amy didn't feel well, and after a few days she woke up paralyzed from the head down. It took time before they realized she had Guillain Barre syndrome which had caused the paralysis. While Amy was trapped in her body, all she could think of was how she would recover and go back to being the mother she was and the wife she wanted to continue being for her spouse.

After a year of treatments and therapies, Amy is doing better. Her rebuilt shoe collection is unworn as she was left with dropped feet which means that she has to walk with a brace and sneakers, most probably for the rest of her life. The reason I mentioned the shoe collection was because she was tested in an area that she felt defined her. That is, how she looked and how she presented herself in the world of fashion and business. However, it was when she lost everything to the fire, and lost the ability to wear the beautiful shoes because of illness, that she realized what really defined her was motherhood and her partnership with her husband.

Amy is grateful to be thriving, enjoying her family and her business, and her second spectacular collection of shoes are a reminder of what was lost and also what was gained. It reminded her how grateful she is for all her blessings. She found the gratitude within the adversity.

Living in gratitude is not just sitting once a day or once a week and taking note of things that happened. A true attitude of gratitude is appeasing your anger when hardship happens because you understand that there within the test, the trial, and the tribulation is something magical, something to be grateful for that you are yet to see.

Gratitude helps you calm your mind, appease your soul, and think more clearly about your situation as a whole and not as a sound bite. You are able to see the miracles in your life. When you see them, you understand that many more are possible. You also see that you deserve these blessings, which in turn helps with self-compassion, the next golden nugget.

**AN ATTITUDE OF GRATITUDE IS GOLD.**

## CHAPTER FOURTEEN

## Golden Nugget #9
# SELF-KINDNESS

*A moment of self-compassion can change your entire day, a string of such moments can change the course of your life* – *Christopher Gremer*

When most people think about self-love, they immediately see themselves with some kind of mask on their face, lavish comfy robes, manicures and pedicures, and a few shopping bags of their favorite brands under their arms. But these fun activities, despite being amazing, relaxing, and surely needed at times, don't provide long-lasting joy.

You can have a massage and the hour is unreal, you feel completely relaxed until you put on your clothes, go to the parking lot, and have to confront traffic. Your manicure feels great and looks beautiful until it starts peeling while you are at the drying station because you hit your nail on the dryer (filled with embarrassment you don't ask for it to be fixed).

Shopping is another double-edged sword. Hopefully, you like yourself in the mirror - but how often do you go to the store, only to get more aggravated that nothing fits you like they do the models on the covers of magazines.

These are maybe worst-case scenarios, but when was the last time that you did any of these activities that you remember it kept you happy for days, weeks, or months? This type of self-love is important and occasionally needed, but it is far from what can lead us to attain successful long-lasting joy. Self-kindness is different.

I often think of the way we relate to our friends in comparison to the way we treat ourselves. When was the last time you told your friend that she is fat, ugly, unaccomplished, lazy, and undriven? I think I can say with all certainty that we would never speak this way to those we love and care about. Actually, we may fib at times, telling them, "You can do anything you put your mind to!"

The truth is no one can do just anything because all of us have different talents. I could not sing, even if you set me up with the most amazing music coaches on the planet. I wish I could, but that is not something that I have the talent for and that is okay. However, we encourage our friends with their dreams, wants and likes; we want to be supportive and show them that we believe in them and even if we exaggerate at times, we really just wish them the best, and we cheer them on; we want them to succeed.

However, when we talk to ourselves, it is like we are talking to our worst enemy and we are that bully in school who we despised. We have no qualms about looking at ourselves in the mirror and bashing our behavior, or our lack of control at the dinner table or in between meals; we have no shame in putting ourselves down with harsh and painful words.

How often we complain about people's insensitivities online! People hide behind their screens and are brutally honest or just brutal and they say things online that we feel are underserving and just wrong. They speak like that to people they don't really know, love or respect. When we witness those people, we are appalled by their words and lack of tact and sensitivity. Then again, we speak to ourselves like that day in and day out, convincing our unconscious mind that we are less than, or underserving, unqualified, and just plain not good enough.

How can we expect anyone to respect us as individuals, parents, siblings, children, workers, or friends when we don't respect ourselves with the same dignity and respect we wished others would give us? It is time to start a movement for self-compassion. #ilovemyself, #irespectmyself, the list would go on and on.

I am worthy. I am enough. I am beautiful no matter my size, color, and hair texture. I am capable. I have talents. I am also critical of myself, as I expect a lot because I know I have talents and gifts I must use; but I am kind at all times.

"Miriam you can do better, you can love more, be calmer, be more tolerant and for sure be more patient... But Miriam you are smart, and accomplished and fast, and generous, and giving, and understanding and loving..."

Do you get the gist? When I tell myself that I need to improve, I do it with kindness, and I also tell myself that I have what it takes to grow and become better. I feel so privileged that I was given so many talents. I show gratitude for being gifted these talents, I don't need to hide and not take the space that I am supposed to take.

But, with privilege comes responsibility. Anyone who thinks that privilege means that we have it easier is mistaken. Privilege means a responsibility to use their talents for the good; we have something that was given to us, and there are conditions attached to these gifts.

Nancy was one of the first women I interviewed and when she approached me with her story, she did so via email. She described her childhood and then her adulthood and I couldn't believe that one person would have to go through so many difficult ordeals in one lifetime.

She had been abused by her father and brothers, she had difficult and bad marriages, she had one son born with many issues including blindness, she had gone through cancer and the list is really long. But there was something exciting and amazing about Nancy and that is her recognition of her amazing talents, abilities, and becoming successful and happy, despite her past.

Nancy knows and is fully aware that she is a very creative, talented photographer, amazing with decorating, smart, and knowledgeable. She is not afraid to have and share her opinions with the world. You would never believe that she had gone through so many devastating and soul-crushing tragedies. I believe that Nancy spoke kindly to herself throughout it all; like a loving supporter and cheerleader. She was able to speak the words others didn't, and today she is strong, energetic, and a conqueror, talking life by the horns and being her best self.

It is time to look within to notice and appreciate all that we were given as gifts, and then realize that we have obligations to use these gifts for the good and expect higher and greater things from ourselves. But we cannot attain greatness if we constantly put ourselves down and speak to our inner self like we are trash, like the pottery that has been broken and is not deserving of being mended.

For those who were bestowed the prize of parenthood, you know that each child has some talents and strengths, and some have less of those and more of others. But you don't say, "Well... Johnny is not musical, and Maria is super slow, so I will love them less." You say, "While Maria is slow moving, she is the kindest, softest, most delicate human I know, and I love her so much." Isn't it true that even when we acknowledge weaknesses in our children, we are so attuned to their strengths and we choose to focus on those?

Well, if we are truly God's children and believe that He is perfection and all His creations are perfection, how could you say that you are less than perfect? You see nature and animals and body parts and how everything works; how the sun rises in the morning and goes down when we need to go to sleep; everything was created with so much love and thoughtfulness, why would you think that you are anything less than perfect?

Maybe the issue is a lack of understanding of what perfection is.

In western culture, beautiful models are the ones who are very symmetric, with perfect-looking faces. We look for symmetry and we look for things that are just so, but Kintsugi is actually an art that celebrates imperfections. It teaches us that the most perfect, valuable bowl, dish, or vase is that one that was broken and mended.

Kintsugi highlights the brokenness because perfection is

achieved through the process of putting it back together. Look at nature. Can you imagine if all the plants and flowers were all even, all the same? Look how the variety, the different sizes, colors, dimensions and shapes are all perfect in nature. We are so accepting that nature is not symmetric, that nature has so much variety, but we are less accepting when it comes to humanity.

In nature there are animals of all colors and shapes, and we don't discriminate against them, and they don't discriminate against each other. Some animals gain more weight and we love them just the same. I know my dog, Lacey, is not watching her waistline and she is just as amazing as when she was trim and fit. I love her the same and she hasn't complained.

Why are we so hard on ourselves? Where did it come from that it is okay for us to bash ourselves this way? I really think that we should be ashamed of how we can so easily put ourselves down: the way we talk to ourselves, should not be harsh and unaccepting.

*Are you willing to treat yourself as you treat those you love?*

*Are you willing to stop this degrading and demeaning behavior?*

If you have the tendency to put yourself down when you are in front of the mirror, how about putting up sticky notes to remind yourself of all your strengths and that you are special; and say these things out loud as you are getting dressed. Or get rid of the mirror all together. If the time that you put yourself down is when you enter your kitchen and you see the dirty dishes; instead of calling yourself a slob, you could say: I am so grateful for the food that feeds my family. I am happy to tackle this mess today and work on a plan to get everyone involved in keeping the house tidier.

Becoming a better and more successful individual begins with your own self-talk. Be kind and loving and attentive to your personal needs. Be kind to your sensitive heart.

Self-compassion is extending love, compassion and understanding to one's self when there is a perceived inadequacy, failure, or general suffering. Kristin Neff has defined self-compassion as being composed of three main parts – self-kindness, common humanity, and mindfulness.

SELF-KINDNESS: Being kind, loving and warm toward ourselves when dealing with pain or personal shortcomings, instead of ignoring them or using hurtful words and self-criticism.

COMMON HUMANITY: We must recognize that suffering and personal failure is part of the shared human experience. We all go through it. There is nothing embarrassing about it, it is the process through which we grow and become better humans.

MINDFULNESS: Creating balance between negative emotions so that feelings are not suppressed, but also not taken out of proportion. Negative thoughts and emotions are observed, recognized and then moved and replaced with peacefulness. Mindfulness is a non-judgmental state in which individuals observe their thoughts and feelings as they are.

What we need to remember is that we must treat ourselves as we treat all the ones we love, and always ensure our words and thoughts are positive and not destructive. Don't be shy to compliment yourself, to point out your strengths, and acknowledge the wins you achieve. You are worth the kindness!

**WORDS CAN BUILD UP OR DESTROY A PERSON.**

Dr. Masaru Emoto studied the changes that speech, feelings, and prayer have on the molecular structure of water, being that the human body is 70% water. We can learn from his studies how speech and feelings affect our molecular structure as well. In essence, we can see that the changes that occur are both emotional and physical.

In his New York Times bestselling book, *The Hidden Messages in Water*, Dr. Emoto explains how water reacts to positive thoughts and words and that polluted water could be cleaned through prayer and positive visualization. The thought that through kindness, prayer, and positive visualization, we can also "clean" ourselves of the "pollution" caused by mean words and thoughts is incredibly empowering.

Based on Dr. Emoto's findings, many tests with rice have been made. Rice is placed in glass jars and labeled with kind words such as love and harmony... and others with mean words such as hate. People spoke daily for 60 seconds using words that aligned with the labels. Within days, signs of mold were clear in the jars with the rice, while the ones where words of love were shared reacted in a positive way.

You can find many of those videos on YouTube and you can try this at home. Once you realize the power of words in such a tangible manner, you will have an easier time adjusting how you speak to people, especially when you speak to yourself.

How we speak to ourselves has tremendous power in how we react and who we become. When we are extended loving words, it makes us grow and thrive, become better and stronger, while negative words destroy us; they crush our self-esteem, our self-love, and our ability to believe in the changes we want to implement.

We have a choice in how we interact with ourselves and by now, most of us need to work hard to break a bad habit of talking to ourselves in a way we would never dare to speak to a friend. We are each blessed with a different set of talents and extraordinary qualities and abilities. We have amazing experiences and incredible tests and hardships. Not one person is better than the other.

Take today to commit to being kinder and more loving and forgiving to yourself. Be mindful to use words with care, love, acceptance, and kindness. Pay attention to how you interact with yourself within your mind. Notice how you relate to your accomplishments, choices, and challenges.

> *We either have a problem or we have a challenge.*
> *We are either punished or we are tested.*
> *We are either breaking or we are rebuilding.*
> *We are either dumb or we are learning.*
> *We are either struggling or we are conquering.*

It can't be both and we need to decide which group we belong to. In so many of the interviews I have conducted, it was clear to see that the words of kindness spoken to women who could have ended up a complete mess, were what actually lifted them up to the successful warrior that they became.

If you believe in God, you know that he has created the world and man with words, you know that kings have conquered lands with words, you know that lives have been saved by the grace of kind words. If you want to thrive and rebuild and become the Kintsugi person you are meant to be, let me be the first to tell you: Self kindness and kind speech is gold.

SELF-KINDNESS IS GOLD.

CHAPTER FIFTEEN

Golden Nugget #10
## ACTS OF KINDNESS

Kindness in words creates confidence. Kindness in thinking creates profoundness. Kindness in giving creates love. — *Lao Tzu*

There are so many times in life that we can go back and see ourselves fall into sadness and disappointment. There are dreams not achieved, jobs lost, illness, divorce, for some - abuse, and many other hardships. The list is long. You can see pain and challenges everywhere; no one is immune. But we all have the power to make a choice to be happy; and frankly, I believe we have the obligation to use this ability.

When I reflect on my past, I see many moments when life took me for a loop. There were times that I just didn't have the tools to comprehend my trajectory and what the next wise steps would be for me to take, leaving me wondering, questioning, and doubting. I think that is a very normal first step when being affected by difficult changes.

Having been raised in a strict European home by parents who gave great importance to education and knowledge, and who had very high standards of ethics and integrity, it did not leave much room for the mundane or the silliness of youth. I was instilled with the force to grow up fast, mature, and be resourceful. I felt I needed to become independent so that I could spread my wings and grow into the person I knew I could be.

I knew some of my decisions would make my parents proud. I also knew that some would leave them puzzled, as there had been so many changes in the world that they did not realize or understand. I chose to leave home for high school, flew to a different country and had to learn a new language and fend for myself at a time when there were no cell phones, no emails, no easy way to communicate and I was only 14 years old. It was, at times, lonely and scary; and at other times, it was very liberating. Overall, it helped me to mature quite fast.

I remember once in high school a few friends and I cut class and went to a get-together at a university. Despite being a harmless act, we did break the rules of the school and after being caught we were punished. We were not allowed to leave the dorm that weekend; instead, we had to stay in school. My friends were crying; they were upset and angry. My reaction was quite different. I told them: "Hey, we messed up, and this is the consequences we have to pay, no biggie. Next time we just need to learn how not to get caught!"

My friends looked at me, wondering why I was not upset that I would not be able to go home (my sister's home) for the weekend. I told them, "Let's make the best of it. Let's buy a lot of junk food, sing, and tell stories at bedtime! Let's all put our mattresses in the same room and have a big slumber party!" I remember that conversation as if it were yesterday, and I see that from a young age, I knew that actions have consequences and the next course of action was to make the best lemonade with the lemons we were given.

I met my husband on a blind date. I fell in love at first sight. I also proposed on our third date. He said he needed more time, I told him he had a few more days. And so, one week from our meeting we were officially engaged. Because I lived in a different country and we were both college students, we were apart for most of our engagement. There were no cell phones, emails, Facebook or Instagram. We recorded tapes and sent them to each other via snail mail, which took sometimes two weeks to arrive. Five months after we were engaged, we were standing at the altar entering into what would be the most amazing, beautiful, scary roller coaster of our lives.

Three days after the wedding I got so sick with a very bad case of mononucleosis. This was a hint of what was to come. There were four insanely hard pregnancies, deliveries that were dangerous, one where I even ended up in the ICU. There have been health scares, losses, and grieving.

There have been financial woes, moves, and numerous tests of faith and strength. Yet, nothing prepared me for my husband's stroke. Nothing prepared me for a person who was always thin, health-conscious, and extremely careful with what he ate, to be diabetic, have hypertension, and be on a daily cocktail of medicines (and not the holistic type). The stroke changed our entire reality, but because he looks well physically, no one understands how it affects our daily lives, technically and emotionally. And most of the time the spouse is overlooked.

One month after my husband had his stroke, I lost my father. Although he had been sick for many years, it seemed that the end came fast and it was unexpected. That time in my life I needed my husband to help me deal with this huge loss and yet, he was unable to support me as he was still dealing physically and emotionally with the aftermath of his stroke.

After so many ups and downs in my life, I felt that this time God exaggerated, and I was sure to share that with Him. But obviously he had a plan that I am not privy to. Like the iceberg, there was so much that I don't know and so much that was hidden from me.

I learned that being humble and accepting that we are not able to understand why things happen and how the world is run puts us in a place of acceptance. But true joy is not residing in acceptance; to feel true joy requires you to move to a place of progress, it requires a belief that this is for the best. True joy resides in acts of kindness and passing the messages onto others.

I again had a choice to make. Am I a victim of my circumstances? Am I going to be in the "poor me" spot and feel bad that things changed in a way that doesn't suit me? Or am I going to grab onto life and fight until I have no power left in me? Until my very last breath?

I envisioned my life on a certain path. Despite knowing that there would be ups and downs as there always were, the joy I had in my heart, the Joie de Vivre was enough to bounce me back from the dips I encountered. I never steered too far away from the excitement I felt about living.

That is, until my life took a U-turn, and no one came to save me. Frankly, I believe that even if "they" - whoever that may be - had come, most probably they wouldn't have been able to save me. What I found out through my adversities and the lives of the many women I was privileged to interview is that the journey can be our salvation. The feelings, suffering, process of rebounding, learning, and growing are all necessary parts of our expansion, healing, and living joyfully.

Kindness is the last Golden Nugget that I share with you in this book. I left the best for last. It is my favorite Golden Nugget of all. Every single one of the Thrivers I interviewed, without exception, model this behavior and this book is an example of how I am contributing to my mission.

When you devote time to help others you are no longer the center of attention. Instead of focusing on your sadness, hardships, and tests, you see a bigger world. You see that you can be of service and you can bring joy to someone else, ultimately, giving you lasting joy.

There is nothing in this world that will make you more joyful for longer than being of service, than being altruistic. Some people focus on giving charity by financial donations, but even that doesn't provide the joy of actually giving your time, yourself, your love, and your attention to someone who needs it.

It may be sitting with someone and hearing their story and saying nothing besides shedding some tears. It may be feeding the poor at a soup kitchen; it may be delivering food to the old; it may be sitting in a hospital and reading the newspaper to someone who needs the comfort and company. Kindness comes in many shapes and that is the most amazing part. We can choose what speaks to us, we can choose to extend ourselves with the talents we have been given.

One of my bucket list items was to go to Utah to the national parks, Zion and Bryce. My husband and I went two years ago. As we stood at the edge of the path, staring at the imposing and powerful mountains, I felt tiny in comparison with the world.

That vista gave me a different frame of reference; it put my pains, aches, and problems all into perspective. To me, they seem so big, but in reality, they are a speckle of sand, a drop of water in this vast ocean. Shifting ourselves out from the center, putting others in it, serving them, being of value to others is the purest form of gold.

When people go through their messes and find healing, they understand that the process was leading them to their mission in life, their purpose. The knowledge we acquire through the painful process is invaluable. I have found that many people suffer similar types of experiences, but each story has a slightly different message and certainly a completely different voice based on the person who went through the journey. There are people who need to hear YOUR STORY, YOUR VOICE. They need to hear about your growth, your healing, and your specific message.

The women who thrive and find long lasting joy are the ones who understand that they have something monumental to share. They gain tremendous joy from helping others who are traveling similar paths. Sometimes they manage to save others from a tough journey as they are there to support even complete strangers in their process. These strangers become part of their sisterhood, their chosen family.

This creates purpose to the pain. One of the devastating parts of going through adversity is not knowing what good it does in the grand scheme of things. We want to know why this pain is necessary, how it is helpful and productive, and why life isn't just simple, harmonious and peaceful.

WHY?

The answer is: your message provides healing to others and has the tremendous power of goodness and kindness. When you embrace the challenge to share what you have learned you suddenly hear yourself saying, "Well, if I can help someone with my story, if they can have my support and suffer less, then it was worth it."

Would you ever imagine that you would say that after adversity? Every woman I spoke with said a big fat "YES!" Including me! If you can be inspired by my resilience, if you can be inspired by my tenacity, if you can be inspired by how I survived and then thrived, then it was all worth it.

I would not choose to go through the pain and loss and the grieving, but now that I have, I am proud of who I have become. My life is richer and surely more joyful.

When the person you help hugs you, cries with you, thanks you for your wisdom, for your love and your support, that is long-lasting joy! That is when your mess becomes your message.

There is no fancy bag, expensive jewelry, or spa that can give you the amount of happiness, joy, and fulfillment you get from acts of kindness. When you actually hear yourself say that the pain brought purpose to your life, you know you have completed the last stage of the Kintsugi piece and the gold is in place, beautifying and making you more valuable and more unique than ever before. Now you know what you need to do. Now you are excited about those you can help. That, my friend, is long lasting joy!

For 25 years I worked in a profession that I loved. I felt fulfilled as I was teaching employees about ethics and integrity, something I am very passionate about. But looking back today I was just living. I was working for the money and I was doing well financially for most of those years. Then I got the wind knocked out of me. I say that figuratively (not counting when my lungs actually collapsed in labor), and today after going through my pain, I feel that it gave me purpose. It gave me the best reason for living.

You see, you are my reason for living: your joy, your well-being. Pain does not discriminate and there is nothing wrong with you, rather you have been bestowed with the opportunity to find your mission in this world, and through this mission you will achieve the most amazing experiences in your life.

I set out to help one woman at a time when I changed my fashion brand to show the art of Kintsugi. I did not know how many women would understand the concept of my brand and how many would actually care. I knew the clothing would sell and many would enjoy the benefits it provides but I didn't know if I could build a tribe and inspire others to find joy and have hope. With time I received incredible messages, I see that I have helped many. So, my dream has expanded.

I believe that when you say something out loud you are accountable for it. I said it on social media that I was going to write my book and I stayed accountable. I now feel that it is time for me to graduate and help many more women, not just one at a time. This book is my commitment. My dream is to give hope to all going through adversity.

Through the interviews I have conducted and will continue to do, I hope to keep sharing with you how to thrive, to create a community that will be supportive and non-judgmental, where woman can come together to cry, laugh, hear each other out, and share techniques that work for them.

I want to create a place where you can feel safe and be loved for no reason other than that you are a fabulous, special person in the middle of a trajectory of challenges that will lead you to the most beautiful of places. The place where you know and understand why you are here and the power you have to practice kindness and help others.

I CHOSE JOY.

There is no shame in being sad and broken, there is no shame in getting help; we are all fighting a fight, we are all struggling with something. The people in your life who judge you harshly and don't give you the benefit of the doubt don't need to be front and center.

Surround yourself with people who are cheering for you, who are willing to give you a hand when you need it, who are proud to see your growth. If social media is causing you anxiety, tune out this fake comparison vortex. Focus on the birds, the trees, the sand, and the wind: the energies and the kindness and the gifts that are bestowed upon you.

Pain is a sign of growth, and there is no way but to go through it. Don't stay in the pain for too long, don't stay in the victim stage; strive to become a Thriver because it is beautiful on this side of pain. And the next time you are challenged, you will always have the tools you garnered from previous experiences.

I hope you are able to heal and can make your mess your purpose.

CHOOSE JOY.

KINDNESS IS THE MOST VALUABLE GOLDEN NUGGET.

WHEN THINGS FALL APART REMEMBER:
YOU ARE KINTSUGI

BROKENNESS
Sit, for a time, with the brokenness and
grieve for what is lost

MENDING
Make an action plan to put your pieces together

CURING
Time and patience are required when
implementing changes

POLISHING
Feed your life with what brings you joy

GOLDEN
Live a life of kindness, helping those who feel
broken, with your love, wisdom and time, aiding as
they go through their healing journeys

APPRECIATE WHO YOU HAVE BECOME.

## CHAPTER SIXTEEN

# REWRITE YOUR NEXT CHAPTER

You can't go back and change the beginning, but you can start where you are and change the ending.
— *C.S. Lewis*

This is YOUR next chapter. Have you ever considered the thought that you are actually the author of your own story? When you look at it that way, you can decide what happens next! You don't need to keep going on a self-destructive path, being a victim of your circumstances, you can steer your ship in whatever direction you desire. You can carefully plan it, make your own choices, and start today on the journey toward a joyful, fulfilling life

This is YOUR chapter. You ARE the author. Use the space in the next few pages to write what you desire for yourself. Start with your physical health, then your mind and soul. What do you envision for your business or the abundance that you know you deserve?

Write your lofty goals, your fantastic dreams, and exciting wishes. Don't be shy to write down every detail and choose only the best of the best! Write down what you are committing to do to attain these dreams. Prepare yourself mentally to work hard, as the runner prepares for a marathon. Start anew, and be determined to keep going even when the road gets rough.

Set timelines, figure out how you can measure your progress, take time to ensure these goals are realistic. Break them down into smaller and attainable steps.

Only those who know their destination manage to make the proper plan to get there. So, make a plan. What will be your first priority? Get invigorated by the vision of the life you dream to have. Do it because you can, because it is a matter of choice and commitment, and most of all, do it because you are worthy!

YOUR NEW DAY STARTS NOW.

## Rewrite Your Next Chapter

## Rewrite Your Next Chapter

## ACKNOWLEDGMENTS

To God: *"Blessed are You, Lord, our God, King of the Universe, who has granted us life, sustained us, and enabled us to reach this occasion."* I know, without a speckle of a doubt, that without God's infinite love for me, this book would not have come to fruition. And so, I am eternally grateful as I am for my strengths and my flaws, my blessings and my challenges. They all brought me to this day.

To my husband, my beloved, my best friend, my everything: Levi – I imagine that living with someone creative, with a "sparkling" brain, who wants to make all the ideas come true, may not be so easy. I fell madly in love with you the day I met you. I never stopped. I would choose you again! Everyday! I choose you today! Thank God you said YES!

To my four daughters and son in law: And I thought I would be teaching you a thing or two… I never expected that I would be learning, growing and becoming who I am supposed to be thanks to you.

Writing a book is a long journey that cannot be done alone. Each of these people had an instrumental part in making this dream a reality.

To all the women whom I have interviewed for the last two years. My "Kintsugi Ladies," thank you for entrusting me with your stories, for inspiring and empowering me to heal.

To Aviva Publishing and Susan for making this process so seamless. To my editors Annie Preston and Jane Maulucci, for all the commas to break my endless run on sentences and for taking on a manuscript written in English by a foreigner. You are truly brave!

Paul Cummings thank you for saying yes to writing the Foreword of my book. You were hand-picked for what you stand for, for your character, your tenacity, your love of life, and because we have something in common... we both have a lot to say!

To Judy Thureson[1] and April Giauque[2], both "Kintsugi Ladies" who are also published authors and held my hands throughout this process. I couldn't have done it without your support.

Matana Poupko Jacobs you are the epitome of this sentence: "A rising tide lifts all boats." I would need to write another book to explain what you mean to me... But I know you know!

Annette Cohen, my chosen sister. Forever and ever grateful. You were my lifeline in very difficult days and always cheered me on while I was writing! I truly hope you, the reader have an "Annette" in your life!

Fally Klein, you have shared the most meaningful, 11-minute voice note testimonial that made me realize that I am on the right path. And whenever I doubt myself, I listen to it again... I have listened to it many times. Many times! Thank you!

For all the members of the Heal with Gold group, thank you for being there and giving me the opportunity to share what's in my heart.

For the photographers, models, make up artists, stylists, who have volunteered to help my brand because you believed in my message and wanted to be part of it. I am forever grateful.

For all the boutiques who took a chance on a brand with a strong and empowering story. You have no idea how many women shared their healing journey with me after they have purchased a Mikah piece in your boutiques. Thank you!

And last but surely not least, Thank YOU, the reader, I have lovingly thought of you throughout my writing journey, hoping and wishing that this book will help bring more joy into your life. This book is for you!

*If you know someone who could benefit from this message, please share a book with them. You may be responsible for someone's healing, and that my friend is true Joy!*

## In Memoriam
## JACOB DOLINGER
### (1935-2019)

My father passed away on October 27th 2019, exactly one month to the day after my husband's stroke and exactly a year before the publishing of this book. To say that his loss was hard on me would be a huge understatement. My father was my beacon of hope, my mentor, my North Star. He always believed in me. But most of all, he knew how to listen to my doubts, he knew how to validate me, and he knew how to push me forward, so that I would achieve more, grow more, learn more.

My pains hurt him; my wins made him ecstatic. He loved discussing everything from marketing concepts to politics and anything in between. He belly-laughed with much gusto at my funnies. He loved my mother with every fiber of his being and honored her till the very end. He cared so much about humanity. He wanted to make an impact in this world (and he did). He was so regal, elegant in his mannerism and elegant with his words. He was an incredible orator, a true academic, a gentle soul, never looking for honor that he so deserved. His students called him Professor even when they became judges; his clients called him Dr., I called him Papi.

Today I woke up at 5 am, eager to write the acknowledgments of this book. As I struggled to keep my eyes open, I thought about a lifetime of 5 a.m.s when my father was reading, learning, and praying. He never stopped until the end. I am so lucky to have had such a role model. Papi, I know you are proud of me as you sit in the highest of heights!

When my father passed away there was one sentence in Hebrew that I was told that brought me some consolation. The sentence was: *"May your father be a Melitz Yosher for you and the entire family."* Melitz Yosher is one who speaks in someone else's defense. The word *Melitz* in Hebrew has three literal meanings:

1. An interpreter
2. One who speaks or writes in an eloquent and beautiful style (from the word "melitzah" which means flowery, poetic language)
3. One who recommends or speaks well of someone ("lehamlitz" means to recommend).

I have no doubt that my father is a *Melitz Yosher* for me and my family, but I equally have no doubt that my father is poetically recommending some major healing with gold for this entire generation. I know we couldn't have anyone better to be fighting for this cause.

# ENDNOTES

### CHAPTER TWO
1 http://bit.ly/SeanBKintsugi

### CHAPTER SIX
1 www.lorettasayers.com
2 Cathy Studer, Author of Broken to Beautifully Whole

### CHAPTER EIGHT
1 Gen Saratani www.urushi.info/kintsugi
2 You can learn more about Ali on Instagram @alilevinedesign and on her Podcast Everything with Ali Levine

### CHAPTER NINE
1 Heal with Gold www.healwithgold.com

### CHAPTER TEN
1 Heal with Gold Course can be found at: www.healwithgold.com
2 April Tribe Giauque shares her escape story in her book "Pinpoints of Light"

### CHAPTER ELEVEN
1 Sycamore Tree Project - https://prisonfellowship.org.au/programs/sycamore-tree-project/
2 www.projectlolo.org Leslie has started a nonprofit that donates prosthesis in third world countries to children in need. She has also written a children's book Lolo's Superpower

### CHAPTER TWELVE
1 Madeleine Black, Author of Unbroken
2 More on Jacqueline DePaul at www.yellowbrickrunway.com

### CHAPTER THIRTEEN
1 World Health Organization: www.who.int
2 www.cdc.gov

### ACKNOWLEDGMENTS
1. Judy Thureson, Author of Beautiful Tragedy
2. April Giauque Author of Pinpoints of Light and Out of Darkness

# You could do it alone...
# But why would you want to?

# Build Resilience, Mend Brokenness and Experience More Joy!

Heal with Gold is a hands-on experience and visual course that will help you through your journey. You will get:

- 8 modules containing multiple videos each
- In depth workbook with assignments to guide you through the process
- A fun hand-on especially for visual learners
- Custom meditation with each module
- A private community with weekly live Q&As
- 2 Free months of membership at the end of the course
- Many amazing surprises and bonuses that will blow your mind!

**www.healwithgold.com**

# JOIN OUR FREE COMMUNITY

## A rising tide rises all boats

Come join our amazing supportive and loving FaceBook community!

**The HEAL WITH GOLD FaceBook group is a great place for you if:**
- Interested in learning from speakers who have experienced adversity and thrived
- Want to be part of a loving supportive community
- You need a space to open up and not be judged
- You want to be empowered and inspired by incredible people
- And you agree to keep politics, religion, hate speech, divisive subjects, profanity out of the group

This group is for women only, so we can freely discuss women's issues. The free lectures are available to all on YouTube at www.youtube.com/mikahfashion. Subscribe today!

**www.facebook.com/healwithgold**

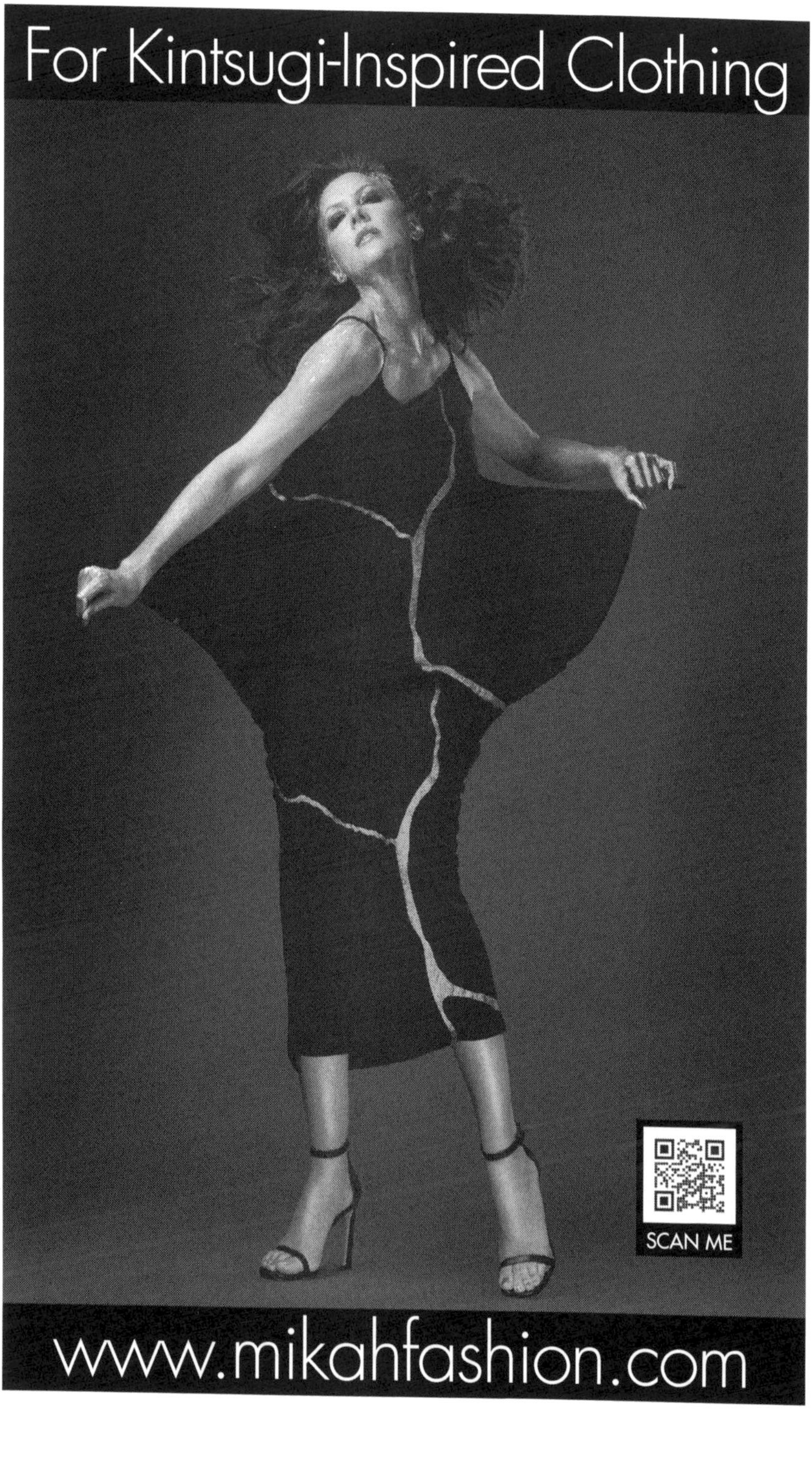


model: @yellowbrickrunway photo @lesleypedraza

## BOOK CLUB QUESTIONS

1. Did you know about Kintsugi prior to reading Heal with Gold? What do you think about the art?
2. How do you relate to the connection between mending broken pottery and mending broken hearts?
3. Do you agree that we should view scars as badges of honor as opposed to something we should hide? Explain.
4. Has this book affected how you go about your life? If so, in what ways?
5. Did you connect with any of the thriver's stories shared? If so, whose?
6. Have you tried any of the golden nuggets in your life? How has it impacted you?
7. What are some passages that particularly affected you? How?
8. Do you think the author succeeded in what she set out to do?
9. What is the most important point the author makes in this book?
10. Does this book change how you see other people? If so, how?

Made in the USA
Columbia, SC
30 October 2020